A RIDER'S READER

EXPLORING HORSE SENSE, SCIENCE & SENTIMENT

MADDY BUTCHER GRAY

Wasteland Press

www.wastelandpress.net
Shelbyville, KY USA

A Rider's Reader:
Exploring Horse Sense, Science & Sentiment
by Maddy Butcher Gray

First Printing – April 2014
Paperback ISBN: 978-1-60047-954-0
Library of Congress Control Number: 2014936144
Cover and author photo by Shepherd Waldenberger

Printed in the U.S.A.

0   1   2   3   4   5   6   7   8   9   10   11   12   13

To the horses, wordless readers.

We need another and a wiser and perhaps a more mystical concept of animals. Remote from universal nature, and living by complicated artifice, man in civilization surveys the creature through the glass of his knowledge and sees thereby a feather magnified and the whole image in distortion. We patronize them for their incompleteness, for their tragic fate of having taken form so far below ourselves. And therein we err, and greatly err. For the animal shall not be measured by man. In a world older and more complete than ours they move finished and complete, gifted with extensions of the senses we have lost or never attained, living by voices we shall never hear. They are not brethren, they are not underlings; they are other nations, caught with ourselves in the net of life and time, fellow prisoners of the splendour and travail of the earth.

Henry Beston
The Outermost House

I don't cotton to no church with walls or bylaws,
But I get down on my knees for Nature.
Take them horses. Why, they deliver homilies every day.
Straight shooters. Nothing thorny.
It's just a matter of knowing their vernacular and showing up.
Not just Sundays but every day.
And, heck, my ass always felt better in a saddle than in a pew.

A. B. McCormick

FOREWORD

People want to do right by their horses. I believe this to be true. After twenty years of doing my part to make the world a better place for horses and their humans by giving people alternatives to doing what they have always done, I still believe that a continuing education is the answer.

The complete definition of the word *horseman* includes not only 'a person who is skilled in riding a horse' but also a person who 'owns, breeds, trains, or tends horses.' Pretty much covers the gamut, doesn't it? But how do we learn what is best for our horses in their training and in the whole of their LIVES? Our horses did not choose to be in our care. We chose them. We are responsible for their well-being, both physical and mental.

Educating humans, however, can be a tall order. Some people learn by observation, others through reading, and many of us through the age-old tradition of trial and error. Unfortunately, while so many of us are open to ideas about how to ride and build a relationship in the saddle, we overlook all the pieces that led to our being up there.

Maddy Butcher Gray's new book, *A Rider's Reader*, covers the spectrum of teaching methods without being a purely instructional book. Her essays of personal experiences made me feel as if I were along for the ride, encountering the challenges and joys of rides through the Maine forests, the hills of Utah, and the wilds, yes wilds, of Iowa. Her interviews with noted horse people describe their lifetimes of experience, thoughts to chew on, and ideas to try—all new lenses to look through to better evaluate our horse keeping and training.

Perhaps most exciting to me is the section on Evidence-Based Horsemanship, a way to scientifically understand what is best for our horses on all levels. It's based not on mere opinion, or misguided traditions, but on empirical science. These are practical insights that will make your horses happier, healthier and more trainable, and that happen to apply to the entire horse world. So don't let the word "science" scare you off.

This compilation can be enjoyed on many levels. I believe it will pull you in and take you along for an educational ride.

Emily Kitching, Editor
Eclectic Horseman Magazine

CONTENTS

INTRODUCTION

In 2008 from my rural home in Maine, I launched the online magazine, *NickerNews*. It had all of three articles. The first newsletter went to sixteen readers. Now, there are hundreds of articles and blog posts. There are advertisers, sponsors, and guest columnists. There are awards and a second website, *BestHorsePractices*. It's been quite a ride.

My goals with *NickerNews* were twofold: sharing news and opinions while fulfilling an itch to write. Call it a journalist's craving; I'd spent many years as a reporter and missed it dearly.

For me, *A Rider's Reader* provides a chance to step out of the saddle and look back.

For you, *A Rider's Reader* provides insight into one woman's journey with horses. Like your journey, it has delightful and dreadful moments. Like your life with horses, it's full of pain, work, love, and learning. This book is not a memoir or a reporter's clips folder, but it has elements of both. Think of it as an eclectic grab bag of experiences, reflections, and research.

A Rider's Reader is ordered from light to heavy then back to light. In other words, it begins with more personal anecdotes and works toward more serious topics before ending with fiction. There is a rough chronology to the entries, as I've traveled and gained and lost herd members.

In the opening chapters, you'll read about outrunning a powerful thunderstorm, swimming with horses, ponying trials, and outlasting winter's challenges. It covers life in Maine, Iowa, and Utah.

Read features on and interviews with Kyla Pollard, Bryan Neubert, Elijah Moore, Randy Rieman, Ben Masters, Leslie Desmond, among others.

There is a chapter devoted to Evidence-Based Horsemanship (EBH), an umbrella term and book by Dr. Steve Peters and Martin Black. I helped the pair with the book's manuscript and covered many EBH events.

Read science reviews and critique on acupuncture, barrel racing, rider weight, bolting, and many more.

Discover what happens to Lily and Jean on their Montana ranch. Read about Oscar and his pair of stalwart donkeys in the French countryside. Read about the retired circus pony, Button, a story originally submitted to the Three Minute Fiction competition on National Public Radio.

The select stories and reports have been chosen from hundreds more, available on *NickerNews* and *BestHorsePractices*.

I hope you enjoy them.

Happy reading. Happy trails. And stay in touch.

ONE:
Life at the Barn &
On The Trail

HONEY & ME

As a kid, I was pretty clueless about horses and riding. My mom and grandma taught what they could to a stubborn but enthusiastic girl. Mom sent me to English lessons for a while. I can still hear the drone of the instructor's voice across the dirt of the outdoor ring: "Heels down. Toes up and in. Shoulders back. Hands lowered…"

When I was twelve, I was invited to take care of Honey, a Welsh pony. She lived up the road from my home in Harpswell, Maine. Honey's owner was going to college. I'd do everything but pay the bills. Pretty nice arrangement.

Honey and I had great rapport. We rode several times a week in the woods and fields of Harpswell Neck. Mostly on our own for hours at a time, we'd ride south along the now defunct Navy pipeline. Riding bareback, I got tossed every other ride. When I relaxed and got distracted, Honey would move laterally, on the pretense of shying at something in the brush. It was a little game she liked to play, I'm sure.

Rides were fun, alright. When I called her from the field, she'd come running. It wasn't for grain. It was for the good time. It was for my girlish affection and our clumsy camaraderie.

More than three decades have passed, but that's what I was feeling yesterday as I set out my saddle for another ride. The horses took notice and gathered around.

"You gonna take me?" they each seemed to ask.

I'm pretty sure they don't care that I ride a bit better than I did as a twelve year old. They're just interested in the good time.

INTRODUCING THE HERD

M̶eet the current herd, in order of typical rank:

Brooke – 14.2 hands. Bay quarter horse. 14 years old (or so).

The alpha mare came to me from a rescue agency and had a history of neglect (being crammed into a stall with three other horses for years). She's the most food aggressive horse I've ever had. She's got bright eyes and can be smart and willing. She can also throw tantrums.

Jodi – 15 hands. Paint. 5 years old (or so).

Jodi came to us from Wisconsin as an untouched tank. Wide and willing, she's curious, strong, and will be a challenge for us as we get her under saddle. She's quickly worked her way up the chain of command and sits at No.2 but can sometimes be out-maneuvered by Shea.

Shea – 15.3 hands. PMU (half quarter horse, half Belgian). 13 years (or so).

Shea was imported from Canada as a Premarin foal. (Premarin foals or "PMUs" are offspring of mares used to produce "Pregnant Mare Urine" which is synthesized for a human menopausal drug.) She had at least three owners before coming to me with little experience under saddle, but she's developed into a sensitive lug and reliable, willing partner. She's not fast or agile but sure is sweet. She's marvelous at ponying other horses, and I often take advantage of her pulling genes for fun or for a job.

Peppermint (Pep) – 13.2 hands. Paint pony of unknown lineage. 14 years.

Her former owners were exasperated by her bolting, spooking, not wanting to be caught, and for her steadfast refusal to assume the role of children's pony. What an incredible go-to girl! She has a well-established reputation of smarts, speed, attitude, and endurance. As long as you stay off the reins and stay ready for sudden movement, you'll have a fantastic time.

Comet – 15.3 hands. Paint. 10 years.

When my significant other, Steve, acquired Comet, she was wild and could not be ridden. Since then, she's been patiently developed as a graceful, strong trail horse. She's near the bottom of the herd rank, which may explain how at ease she is on her own. She's a bit of a prima donna whether in the pasture or on the trail; she acts dainty and likes to have things just so.

Jolene – 15.3 hands, beautiful black and white molly mule from Missouri. 6 years (or so). She was acquired from an Iowa friend who bought her at auction. It wasn't working out; the mule was often frightened and had a bolting tendency.

෨ – ෴

A few practical and philosophical notes: At my barn, we're into long-term relationships, potential over pedigree, second chances for troubled horses, and letting horses be horses with minimal management. Like so many of you, these ideas continue to evolve as I learn more as a person, journalist, and horsewoman.

HERD DYNAMICS

Why did it take so long to realize I was part of the herd? It dawned on me one bleary morning as I trudged out to toss hay.

I witnessed the trickle-down dynamics as the horses shuffled for position in the new order. I moved Brooke. Brooke moved Shea. Shea moved Pep. Pep moved Comet. It was a fluid pecking order. Everyone knew her position and I was at the top.

Over the next few days, I paid more attention to their movements when I arrived. They didn't *need* to move the next horse down the line. They seemed to do it simply to assert their new position, after I'd inserted myself at the top.

Ever watch a really good tennis player against a lesser player? The good player barely moves as he hits his shots. The lesser player chases those shots all around the court and uses tons of energy.

That's what higher ranked horses do too. They move others without lifting a hoof. All it takes is a pursing of the lips, pinning of the ears, or swish of the tail.

BARN TIME

Lately the barn has been my church. It's where I come for peace of mind and distraction from the less pleasant aspects of my world. It's where I appreciate and feel appreciated.

During the summer months, I like to plop myself down on a wooden box and kick back with the horses. The tack room radio plays, but what I hear most clearly is the sound of the horses chewing hay, the swishing of tails, the relaxed steps to the water, the draw and dribble of their drinking. Ain't it musical?

The smells are therapeutic, too. My *NickerNews* sweatshirt reads "Your Horsesh*t is My Aromatherapy." But it's true, ain't it? Horse folk understand.

And it's not just horseshit, but horse breath and horse coat. I've noticed that my pony, Pep, emanates the nicest, most horsey smell. Each one smells like a horse, of course, but different horses smell distinctive.

I linger at the barn more in the summer. It's warm and light enough to see. But even when wearing five layers, I often hunker down on the stoop to pause. Just for a moment, I watch their frosty breaths and peer with them into the darkness. And be thankful.

BULLIES & UPSTARTS, I

I've spent summers ponying horses to the neighbor's field every day. Trixie, a little thirty-year-old Shetland was one of them. On occasion, I would catch Trixie biting at the belly of the horse I was riding.

What? This bottom-of-the-totem-pole pony seemed to be taking delicious, vengeful nips at the Top Dog. My riding horse couldn't check her, being under my control and all. Trixie knew this.

I got a good chuckle out of this natural and personal opportunism. I thought it was a unique moment. Not so.

Trixie moved to a friend's farm, and Peppermint Patty moved to my place and replaced her at the bottom. Now, I ride Shea and pony Peppermint and another horse to the field. I caught this clever pony pulling the same move.

If you could diss your local bully without fear of payback, wouldn't you?

II

People, dogs, cats, horses: When it comes to dominance and bullying, they're pretty much the same.

I saw the other day how some guy launched his willing girlfriend in his homemade trebuchet. I exclaimed to a friend, "What kind of idiot would launch his girlfriend into the air?"

"What kind of idiot girlfriend would agree to it?" was his reply.

Indeed.

I watched this morning as my eight-pound cat reigned supreme over the water bowl. He wasn't the least bit thirsty. He just felt like asserting himself.

Ruby, my sixty-pound black lab, waited tentatively until the cat got tired of it and sauntered off to laze in the sun.

I got a call from my friend, Rick. He's been caring for Trixie. The little Shetland was at the bottom of the totem pole at my farm. Now, reports Rick, she's pushing around her twelve-hundred-pound pasture mate, Cupcake.

"I sure wish Cupcake would grow a pair," said Rick. "Why is Trixie doing it?"

Because Trixie can. She tried it once. Cupcake gave her no resistance, so she did it again.

III

When we put our own unpleasant feelings onto someone else and blame them for having thoughts that we really have, it's called *projecting*.

So, can horses do it? If so, I surely witnessed it in Comet. She's the most bullied horse in my herd. And I think she gets a little weary and frustrated by this position.

The other day, my dog was hanging out with the horses. She sniffed absentmindedly in the pasture, minding her own business (eating manure, of course). I watched as Comet approached the dog. She stealthily maneuvered around the dog and positioned herself to get the most out of a double barrel kick to the dog's midsection.

I yelled. Comet, seemingly caught in the act, stepped away and skulked off. She tried it again a day later. I'm thinking I should chat with Comet about how targeting the dog won't help how she feels about being at the bottom of the pecking order. Then again, how do I know?

DOGS

Most of us are dog lovers, too. I know this because when I travel barn to barn, dogs nearly always greet me. So, I hope you, dear reader, will indulge me as I embrace some dog memories and moments on these horsey pages.

EULOGY FOR TOM

He is Thomas, Tom, for short. Tom was put down yesterday after a long, love-filled, and productive life. I adopted him when my family and I lived in Ireland.

Funny story: It was a lovely day in the summer of 1996. My three sons (ages one, three, five) and I were walking around St. Stephen's Green in the center of Dublin. St. Stephen's is a ten-acre park surrounded by four lanes of crazy traffic, a commercial district, and a gritty, densely-populated neighborhood.

We were eating cookies and people-watching when this thin, dirty, little mutt bounded up to us. Hungry. Obviously stray. The boys gave him cookies and fell in love with him instantly. Almost as instantly, I made the decision: we'd take him in. But how?

One stroller. Three young'uns. A long subway ride and twenty-minute walk from home. Add this collarless, leash-less dog to the mix? I imagine more than a few Dubliners were shaking their heads as we made our way home with the new family member.

My oldest, Aidan, was charged with pushing his baby brother, Cormick, in the stroller. Beau, the three year old, held my hand. I carried Tom on my other hip. Tom was pretty cool with the idea but still squirmed occasionally. Cormick was not at all impressed with his brother's reckless stroller handling—something to do with slamming into each street curb, I think.

As we approached the Tara Street station, I prepped the boys for the possibility of rejection. "You know, they might not let us on the DART (Dublin Area Rapid Transit) with a dog. That would be really sad, wouldn't it?"

Sure enough, the ticket-taker took one look at us and shook his head, "Not allowed, ma'am."

As if conducted by a chorale director, my sons pined in perfect, pathetic pitch, "Nooo! You can't!" Their pitiful faces would have made any drama coach proud.

The ticket-taker winced and reluctantly waved us through, "But you didn't get on here!" he yelled after us.

Tom came home to our tiny rented house in north Dublin with a cement-walled yard smaller than an American kitchen. Regardless, it was a joy-filled beginning. The boys adored him and he loved them back.

Around the neighborhood, dogs were hardly ever on a leash. Tom was the perfect diplomat: all tail-wagging and pleasantries. One might say he had that Irish gift of gab. A social butterfly. In his fifteen odd years, he was never part of any fight.

I had him checked out and neutered by a local vet. We thought he was perhaps part Jack Russell, part Border collie.

When the kids played in the street (that's where kids play in Dublin), Tom would try to herd them. When we found fields and parks to run in, Tom would cast big circles around his boys and their friends, keeping them all gathered up.

After several months, we returned to the States, and there was no question that Tom would come with us. I shipped him ahead of us, and while we resettled, he stayed with my mother, Sally Butcher.

∽ – ✻

Tom takes a big, strange, and possibly scary trip on a plane. He lands at Logan International Airport where one of the biggest dog lovers ever receives him.

They travel to Maine where he takes up residence with two friendly Labrador ladies, the aforementioned dog lover, and endless woods. No fences. No traffic, just girlfriends and regular meals.

Died and gone to heaven.

It's no wonder then that when he returned to us, he seemed to give me a less than appreciative look. 'You again? I liked your mother better.'

Tom did end up with my mom in 2001. She really liked him, and at the time, I was newly single with three sons. I had two other dogs too.

Mom and Tom made quite a pair. As a dog owner, Sally believes an active life is a good life. He excelled at fly ball and agility. Competitors would ask her about his breeding. Once she said with a straight face, "He's an Irish pub dog." That comment had traction, I'll tell ya.

Tom's specialty in his later years was as a therapy dog. They traveled to nursing homes, schools, and hospitals. Kids read stories to him; Tom listened well.

She recalled a recent trip to Togus, the Veteran Administration Medical Center in Augusta. They were visiting a vet in the Alzheimer's unit. After some time with the gentleman, Sally indicated it was time to go.

"That's OK," said the patient. "But don't take the dog."

My mom told me, "Tom defined what it is to be a therapy dog. He enriched so many lives."

We are so very thankful that this little Irish street mutt came into our lives.

We lift our glasses and wipe tears. Mom speaks for many of us when she says, "It's tough losing your best friend."

LIKE DOG, LIKE PONY

The dog, Belle, and the pony, Peppermint, have a lot in common. They're short. They're smart. And they're the bane of my existence.

Please forgive me as I indulge the parallels that came creeping to mind after a recent outing with Belle. Like the pony, this dog makes me laugh through gritted teeth.

Belle is half basset hound, half dog-next-door. I discovered her from a flyer posted at the local feed store several years ago. I'd never owned a hound. Hounds have a tendency to run off, my mom pointed out. I shrugged.

Such a cute puppy. And I'll train the hound out of her.

Belle has seven-inch legs. Her body, from nose to tail tip, is nearly five feet long. This confirmation suits her well for barging through the underbrush.

We headed out for a walk with the other dogs. Unlike the others (all non-hound dogs), Belle picks her own route, following her nose. We usually don't see her until the end of the twenty-minute walk, when she predictably and faithfully reappears and seems to say, 'I had a great tour around the woods. How 'bout you?'

This time, though, within minutes of her routine departure, we heard yelping. Belle was excited and moving south fast. My first thought was of a porcupine. But her yelps faded quickly. This was a chase, not a cornering. And the chase was on.

We called in the other dogs, and I jogged in the direction of her last yelps. When I listened for her again, the barking was at least a half mile away. Or more.

I stood in the now-quiet woods. Time passed. Then I started hearing her yelps again. Amazingly, they were coming closer and closer. I strained to look through the trees and brush. There, pacing toward me on the diagonal was a beautiful red fox. It crossed my path twenty feet in front of me, kept jogging, didn't break stride, or even bat an eye.

I imagine the fox was having a little fun. His Sunday stroll had turned into a Sunday jog. No big deal. And when he glanced at me, he almost seemed to say, 'Gave her a test drive. Brought her back. You take her now.'

A minute later, an exhausted, exuberant Belle trotted toward me. I took off my belt and looped it through her collar as a leash. She seemed almost thankful that I'd thwarted her pursuit. Like pony and her little escapades, the hound just couldn't help herself.

RIDE-ALONG DOG

If we got another dog, we wanted a ride-along dog; thus, the summer acquisition of Kip, an Australian shepherd from a litter of eight at my hay guy's farm down the road.

Kip's growing up and at six months can outrun nearly everyone. Her speed and wiliness mean I feel more and more comfortable about walking in the pasture amongst the herd with her.

The horses are interested, especially Jodi. The new girl would like to move Kip. Kip would like to move Jodi, and anything else for that matter. She's growing into her form and breed instincts, less intimidated and more curious by the day.

On the last few pasture walks, her herding nature blossomed in full form. She was done with being intimidated and confronted the horses with new authority.

Kip has figured out how to stress the horses alright, and therein lays the problem. While she generally stays clear of danger and knows "Out!" as a command to leave the pasture, she needs improvement to keep her safe and the horses sane.

"Have a good 'down,' a good recall, and a good 'off,'" said Dr. Cynthia Reynolds of Searsport, Maine. "It will save her life in a lot of situations."

For those unused to dog commands:

- Down - Lie down wherever you are.
- Recall - Come to me.
- Off - Leave whatever you're interested in right now.

Aside from working as a veterinarian with acupuncture and chiropractic expertise, Reynolds is also an avid herding dog trainer. She also suggested leashing Kip, walking her around the horses in a calm manner and then leading the horses around Kip. It's important to use a lot of positive reinforcement, always rewarding her for calm, added Reynolds.

Just like horses, the more you extend training to different scenarios, the more likely your dog will behave. "You can have it perfect when it's just you and her, but then you get around livestock or other dogs and it's a different story," said Reynolds. "Take her to different places so it gets really solid. Obedience classes are really helpful."

- ✓ Obedience class
- ✓ Positive reinforcement
- ✓ Field trips

Thanks, Dr. Reynolds.

HORSE TRAINING MANTRA FOR DOGS

Horse trainers like to say, "Make the wrong thing hard and the right thing easy." I embraced the strategy with my dog, Kip, during our most recent training session. In this case, weather lent me a helping hand.

As previously noted, Kip has had a hard time restraining her herding impulse. More than once, this young Aussie has left me breathless and frustrated as she attempted to gather her half-ton charges. It's not just a matter of obedience, of course but one of safety and welfare.

Our goal during today's session was simply to hang out in the pasture, have the horses move around us, and be calm. Simple, you say, but no easy feat for us.

First, we toured the pasture perimeter. It was hot and humid. With her black, thick coat, she warmed up quickly. We moved closer to the horses grazing lazily. I asked Kip to lie down and stay in the shade while I moved with the horses. Being naughty, then, meant getting overheated through movement and sunshine.

For what seemed like the very first time, Kip had an added incentive she could really feel. By doing nothing (against any Aussie's nature), she was successful. What a good pup!

Our education continues.

TWO:

Seasons

FIELD MOMENTS

When summer slips toward fall, nostalgia starts knotting my throat. The wonders of Maine's warm season are fading. I want and need to cherish them and hold them close, as if they were the heating pad to get me through winter.

Sure, there are savored memories of riding and camping with friends, and the small 'aha' moments with better riders and trainers. I'm especially happy with the improved rapport between me and my horses. But what I cherish most are the quiet moments at the field and the coexistence of me, my horses, and everything else out there buzzing around.

I approached the field one evening and started walking through the knee-high grass. Ahead of me, a dozen mature turkeys quickened their pace. Their heads matched the height of the tallest grasses and bobbed along like rosy-grey golf balls floating on the field's surface. It was surreal.

On another day, I caught up with a porcupine as he was bumbling across that same field. I was thankful he hadn't traipsed into my fenced-in area. The girls probably would have felt the need to investigate. And then I would have been investigating a muzzle full of quills.

By the end of July, the field was starting to fill with scads of newly-fledged baby birds—sparrows, bluebirds, and swallows. The fence, of course, was where they perched and called for their parents: *"Feed me! Feed me!"*

On that same fence, I often saw a kestrel. I love raptors and the kestrel is one of my favorites. He was probably eating those baby songbirds. That's life, right?

Cowbirds are beautiful in their plainness and the way they cling to horses. It's an instinct that's amazing to observe.

Mr. Woodchuck and I had several close encounters. He took up residence in the woodpile near where I park my bike. (I bike to the field. Leave the bike. Ride horses home. I bike back home when I drop the girls off each morning.) Mr. Woodchuck was unfazed when I checked out his digs. Three feet separated us, and he stared me down.

Deer tend to move into the field by late afternoon. I don't know what they feel about the horses or what the horses think of them. But I get the sense they like each other's company.

At night, when the horses are back with me at the barn, I often hear coyotes. I love coyotes. But I wouldn't want to see them track down one of my dogs. Later in the month, they got that porcupine, by the way. My neighbor says coyote with muzzles of quills often starve or die from infection. That's life, too.

You can have your reality shows. Life in the field is my kind of real world.

TRAIL RIDE VESTIGES

We were easing off a long trot. As we slowed, Shea and I finally could take our eyes off the trail. We'd been ducking branches and hopping over roots for some time. There, just off the old logging road, was a straight, low stone wall. It enclosed no field and came to an ill-defined end after one hundred fifty feet.

Spotting stone walls is like coming across an old family album. They are treasures from another time. They provide images of how things were and carry me back. In this case, the journey goes back well over a hundred years to when Brunswick settlers worked these parts. They are woods-turned-fields-turned-woods.

What did this wall enclose? What men and women tended this land?

I can ride in an arena for about as long as I can shop in a mall. Thirty minutes and I'm headed for the exit. But trails call me. With deer season around the corner, I cherish them even more.

On this day, we suffered a mile of busy road-riding to get onto these fantastic, old Brunswick tote roads. Generations ago, folks harvested wood and tilled fields here. Now the wide paths are scarcely used outside of hunting season. But they provide my horses and me with hours of escape three seasons of the year.

Stone walls weren't the only sign of yesteryear. I love my native state dearly, but Maine has a serious dumping habit. Old fridge? Old tub? Old sink? Old truck? Just take 'em out back into the woods.

I went to Mt. Ararat School in Topsham, and the quarry behind the high school was full of junk. It was deep. Dozens of cars were turned invisible by its tea-colored waters.

As time goes on. The sinks and tubs and trucks start blending in with the woods. As we walked past an appliance graveyard the other day, it seemed like at some point it stopped being an eyesore and started being almost quaint. Call me a patriotic Mainer, huh?

Everything dumped was decades in its new place. The only new items were Poor Man's Deer Stands—five-gallon buckets.

Civilization could be heard, too, for Interstate 295 hummed in the distance. We rode some more, came to our little highway overlook, and paused to watch all the RVs head south. They blended with the work trucks and regular commuters.

I suppose there is never total escape around here. Humanity will pop up—in the form of an abandoned tub or traffic or a siren in the distance. But what good fortune to ride out the back door. I'll take trail riding here with all its warts and farts.

AUTUMN AND TRAIL RIDING

Many consider autumn the best time of year for riding. Count me among them. Bugs? A non-issue. Weather? Perfect. Horses? Spirited and fit.

In Maine, I got to know my local woods a bit better with some bushwhacking. My late paint, Phoenix, seemed to revel in the prospect of finding new routes, plunging through swamps and pushing through brush toward clearer ground.

Nowadays, Shea is game. But she's so laid back I'm not sure she really discriminates between paths and non-paths. It's all good.

We managed a trip to Andover, Maine, and did some long rides there, using Deb Cayer's place, Memory Lane Vacations, as a base camp. On one ride, we rode for five miles or so, toward Devil's Den. We crossed the Ellis River and its tributaries, loped through fields, took turns leading through long spells of trotting in the woods.

After a few hours, we reached a pretty little meadow, or I should say, yet another pretty little meadow, as they pop up all the time on these routes. We stopped. Off came the bridles and saddles. The girls munched contentedly while we kicked back and soaked up the fading sun.

I thought for sure the horses would be dragging all the way home, but the break brought a new spring to their steps. Or maybe they were simply eager to get back.

AUTUMN IN IOWA

More than New Year's or the beginning of summer, the transition from summer to fall always gives me pause. It's a reflective time as daylight shrinks and animals uproot themselves from summer climes and move on.

Rides are quiet and more subdued but noisy and frenetic in patches. Horses are calmer and more conditioned, but the crisp air combined with new smells and sounds can make them fresh and on edge. The partnership-building and months in the saddle start paying dividends now.

Iowa is an insane avian thoroughfare this time of year. There are clouds, not flocks of birds. Their sounds are so intense that it startles the dogs and horses. If you stop near these masses, or if they linger around you, their thousand-voiced calls make for loud, pleasant, white noise.

Grackles, blackbirds, starlings, and swallows float on invisible roller coasters. They seem to search out and descend on each other, combine in droves, and then take to the air again. They turn a field from brown to black when they land. Telephone poles, trees, and shrubs seem to hold them all, but on closer approach, scores more spring up from the ground and grasses.

Not coincidently, there are hoards of raptors, too. On today's ride, I saw twenty within the hour. There are red-tailed, sharp-shinned, Cooper's, and marsh hawks along with Bald Eagles.

The foliage is duller than in New England. But nice and not without exceptions—some trees perfectly glow with leaves. In June, I was shocked by the bright green hues of Iowa's grasses and planted fields. That landscape palette faded as a summer of heat and drought set in. Now, we have gorgeous reds, yellows, purples, and browns as plants close up shop for the season.

Like Maine at this time of year, there's a refreshing dimension to riding through the woods: you can see. And by that I mean, you can see beyond the next turn. You can see animals before they find cover. You can see nests that birds have left behind.

After deer season (From the way folks here talk, it may be more dangerous and foolish than in Maine, if that's possible.), I'm looking forward to more exploration. With the woods opened up, bushwhacking is more fun. You can maintain a quick pace even if you're wandering, getting kinda, sorta, not really lost.

MAYNARD

It started some years back. My neighbor, Maynard, took a fancy to my horses. When it came time to harvest the corn in his garden, he'd load up the stalks and chug across the yard on his tractor. At the fence, he'd make sure each one got her fair share.

I'd usually meet him to say thanks and to retell him their names, which he'd forgotten since the year before. He liked Shea the best and chided Brooke on her rudeness. Over the course of a few weeks, the horses came to connect his tractor's sound with treats. They'd scurry for position, line up, and wait.

Maynard is one tough guy. At five feet six, maybe one hundred thirty pounds, and turning ninety this year, he might not look it. But a few years back, he woke up with chest pains and drove himself to the Emergency Room. He and his wife, Geneva, life-long vegetarians, raised five children and always maintained a mammoth, meticulous garden. They heat with wood from their property. They were self-sufficient long before it became fashionable.

It's only since the heart attack that his pace has slowed. Still, he visited often, bringing apples, even snowshoeing over in winter's twilight to say hello and offer treats.

Last fall, Maynard was working in his back field when he felt weak and dizzy. His son got him on the tractor cart and took him to the hospital. He'd had a stroke.

I visited him during his long rehabilitation at a Portland facility. He told me he was impatient to get home for Christmas. "If you do, Peppermint and I will come for a visit," I said for encouragement.

It came as no surprise when he defied odds and progressed enough to return for the holiday. We got togged up and headed over. If I hadn't held her back, Peppermint would have showed no hesitation and joined him in his kitchen!

There's official therapy. Many wonderful friends work with their animals to help veterans, children, and countless clients in need. It's incredible work and my hat is perpetually off to them.

Then there's unofficial therapy the rest of us have the privilege of providing every once in a while. Often these quiet visits speak volumes for connecting and raising spirits of those without horses. It reminds us horse owners how lucky we are: Lucky to pay it forward, lucky to have that animal connection for ourselves every day. Having horses can soothe our souls in more ways than one, can't it?

Since December, Maynard has continued to improve. This week, he visited with apples and carrots, albeit with a cane and his daughter's help. The girls heard that familiar engine and lined up. They were thrilled. And so was I.

A SEASON OF THANKS

Friends, particularly horse friends, are the tinsel on my tree. With the help of a friend, I reinvested in riding this year. I devoted time to my more challenging horses. It paid off marvelously. The horses are better and I'm more confident with them. All I needed was encouragement and a skilled rider to help iron out the kinks. Thanks!

Another horse friend made it possible to get away from the farm. We live near each other and know each others' routines and animals. She made trips to the Equine Affaire and *War Horse* possible. Thanks!

Horse friends aren't afraid to get dirty. They'll get up early for you and stay up late. They hold the flashlight as you clean a wound. They sit on the stoop and drink beers and coffees with you. They make plans and dreams with you. They gallop into the wind with you. They spit and curse with you. They help you bury a beloved. Thank you, friends!

CHRISTMAS PARADE IN IOWA

About eight hundred men, women, and children live in Swisher, Iowa. Each December, the city planners organize an evening Christmas parade. Anyone can sign up.

Given Swisher's size, I figured riding in the parade would be like any other evening ride around here—a quiet, mellow affair. Maybe a few folks would stand on the sidewalk with votives, waving. Heck, we can do that! I signed us up.

As the date grew nearer, I took note of significant pageantry preparations. My co-workers at the KaVa House & Café worked for hours in the shop's basement, like Santa's elves, excitedly designing a giant coffee mug to go on top of a borrowed golf cart.

I noticed parade floats in various stages of development on neighbors' front lawns: a nativity float here, a hunter's float there. More decorations along the parade route were added and buffed up.

All this activity made me nervous. Better make a dry run, I thought. For Shea, we first needed to address two new items close at hand:

- Bells: I draped a heavy leather collar of brass harness bells around her neck. They chimed with every step. If she stepped quickly, they rang quickly (and loudly). It took a few spins around the block for her to come to terms with them.
- Lights: I wrapped those bells with red and green, battery-powered Christmas lights. Surprisingly, she had little issue with them after their dazzling introduction.

On the eve of the event, I took Shea by trailer to the post office and had a walk around with her flashing new necklace. We walked past the bar, the general store, the library, and the houses with flashing holiday displays. We stopped by the KaVa to say hello. No problemo.

But on parade night, something tipped me off that it wouldn't be the quiet and mellow outing I had predicted. Maybe it was the Christmas songs blaring over the loudspeaker. You could hear them from a mile away. Maybe it was the fireworks. Maybe it was the people—hundreds of people with lights and loud voices and energy lining Second Street, a veritable vortex of holiday excitement.

Shea pooped. (I let her graze.) Shea snorted. (I let her move and face the music.)

She was the only horse in a ten-float line. We got sandwiched between the KaVa float and the hunter's float, which was looping ZZ Top's "Sharp-Dressed Man" at full volume. As we moved toward that tunnel of spectators, those floats faded away. For a moment, Shea held the spotlight. She pranced. One might even say she rose to the occasion. Happy holidays, all! Thanks for having me, Swisher!

CABIN FEVER

C abin fever struck my farm. It was late and cold. The moon was coming up on the horizon, and there was stillness in the air. Stillness shattered by Brooke's spinning and bucking, anxious for the evening hay toss or just sick of winter?

The energy caught on and before you knew it, all four horses were running furious laps around the two-acre pasture. Their route started at the top of the hill, where they paused and looked over their snow-covered space. I swear one of them said, "Ready. Set. Go." Off they galloped—down the hill, past the round pen, and toward the road.

They must have sensed the smooth, thick layer of ice under the inch of snow. It covers half an acre—a perfect rink of slickness. And for a few laps, they negotiated the turn back to the hill perfectly, despite the slippery subsurface. One after another, they threaded the tight, five-foot alley created by the wood fence on one side and the round pen panels on the other.

I was watching a rider-less Olympic cross country event, full of speed and grace. That is, until the Miss Grace miscalculated.

Among the four, Comet, the slender paint, is the daintiest and prettiest mover. On this day, however, as the others dug in to round the turn for the third time, she slipped and slid on the ice, crashing through two rails of wood fencing.

She got up immediately. Unhurt, she caught up with her herd mates, shook her mane, and trotted in a circle. When they took off for another lap, Comet joined them at a reserved and demure trot, pausing to see if I was bringing hay any time soon.

And they say horses don't get embarrassed.

WINTER'S UPSIDE

I've had an epiphany. Winter isn't the long, subzero trudge toward spring. It's an angelic time of year, perfectly brimming with advantages. I offer you, dear reader, a small sampling:

1. As the snow mounts, all those out-of-reach places and things—the hay loft, spent bulbs on the barn floodlight, Jolly Balls flung into trees, shoes strung up on telephone poles by deviant teenagers—are now reachable.
2. When your horses escape, they're fairly easy to track down.
3. No bugs.
4. No ticks.
5. No sweaty saddle pads to air out (like we're riding anyway, right?)
6. No flooding. We get snow on top of ice. It's real pretty and hides the mess we'll have come mud season.
7. Struggling with your diet? Not to worry. No one (including you) will be able to tell if you've lost or gained any weight under all those layers.
8. Speaking of layers…No need to get out of your PJs to do barn chores. Just throw on those coveralls and barn coat over them.
9. What urine smell? It freezes too quickly to stink. Then you can lift it out of a stall as one big urine patty. Nifty.
10. Manure freezes hard, too. These nuggets come in handy when your deviant teenager decides to surprise you with a snowball fight.
11. Picking hooves is easier. They're usually completely clean OR completely bonded with four inches of ice and snow. Hammer comes in handy here.

12. You feel an extra sense of connection with your horse because you both have mini icicles hanging from your nose and eyelashes.

FROZEN WORDS

The cold is going to my head. Know the feeling? You've been out in the cold for hours, someone starts talking to you and you will agree to just about anything if it means getting warm.

Ten minutes in a warm car and a cup of hot cocoa?? Sure, take my house. Yes, my family says I'm losing it (and they're not talking about the house.)

When I get cold, I can't form words correctly. If I was takking to a powiice officer, I'm shuwah he would wan' to gib me a breaffalyzer tess. And if I could sit in his warm cruiser, I'd be happy to oblige. Seriously, it is challenging to make rational decisions and complete reasonable tasks when you fear your teeth will crack on the next inhale.

And you know when your hands and feet get really frozen and then they start to burn? It is a delectable sensation. Sure, it's painful and kind of nauseating, but after the stinging sensation comes the warm flow of blood back to your fingers and toes. Oooh, hurts so good.

If you wrap your arms around your horse, he or she can keep you warm for a bit. After all, they do regulate themselves a few degrees higher than us. I was riding bareback the other day and didn't want to get off.

BARN TIME AS ESCAPISM

E ven when it's zero, I deeply cherish my barn time.

The other night, I was holiday baking like a mad woman. I set eight mini-bundt pans full of Christmas coffee cake in the oven. They would bake much quicker because they were smaller, I figured.

Thirty minutes later, I calculated they'd be done.

Forty minutes.

In and out of the oven. Toothpick-tested. Finger-tap-test. Still not done.

At fifty minutes, I pulled them out for good. If only! I had to relight the oven when I realized they still weren't done. That's when I set the timer, gave instructions to my son, and headed to the barn to do chores and seek refuge.

Ah, the barn. Ah, my dear horses. What a welcome retreat. Give me a muck rake over a rubber spatula any time.

CHANNELING SUMMER

I t felt almost like summer. I hauled my last load of manure to the pile, stored the wheelbarrow, and placed the rake back in the tack room. The horses watched me move around their space.

I picked up my bottle of beer and sat for a spell on the stoop. Peppermint lipped my collar, investigated, and stayed close. The others milled, coming close to smell and breathe on me.

The stars were out and the moment felt like so many summer evenings, when a pause after a long day lets you soak in the pleasures of horse ownership: the smells, sounds, actions, and energies of these compelling animals.

Almost like summer, except Peppermint was lipping coveralls, not shorts. You could see our breaths. My boots kicked up bits of ice. Those stars were out before dinnertime. Three feet of snow blanketed our surroundings. That beer stayed nicely chilled for an hour.

COLD IS RELATIVE

It being ten degrees, windy, and all, I was starting to piss and moan about the cold until I saw these guys clamming near Strawberry Creek in Harpswell. I may be outside all morning, but I'm not sinking my hands and feet into cold, unwelcoming mud. I know that mud. I grew up trudging across the flats of Middle Bay. That mud clings to you. It gets into the cracks of your skin and tints your hands four shades darker. But I know this from summer months. Then, you could just jump in and swim it off. Staying wet was welcome, not painful.

My friend, Rick, was telling me about winter clamming when he was a kid. "It was a matter of survival," he said. Rick, his father, and brothers went clamming to earn enough to put food on the table.

He remembers clamming one day as a ten year old. His gloves weren't keeping his hands warm enough and he was complaining. His father gave Rick his gloves and he continued on, barehanded. Barehanded!

So, I have respect for winter clammers. I appreciate them showing me that cold, pain, wet, and warm are all relative.

SPRING

Mud season is when one thinks longingly of summer routines, easier horse care, and more riding. It's within our grasp. We can feel it.

First, though, the month-long wading through slop, the stink of the paddock as old manure and hay ripen with the warmer temps, and more water lugging.

The disappearing snow also reveals some lapses in maintenance, that missing shovel, the broken fencing, the long-lost hoof pic.

Spring also reintroduces us to fresh horses. Wouldn't it be nice if we could start off with calm, willing horses and have the more challenging stuff later in the season when we're in shape and more wily? But, nooo, we get the cold turkey challenge of working with fresh horses when we ourselves may be a bit rusty and out of shape.

If the bike had attitude, weighed a thousand pounds, startled at sudden movements and loud noises, then YES! Riding every spring would be just like climbing back on that bike.

We hop back in the saddle and head into the perfect storm of fresh horse, unfit body, and a greater public who hasn't seen a horse on the road since…well, sometime before deer season.

TRAILER TO-DO CHECKLIST

Spring means getting the cobwebs out of training and, literally, your trailer. My friend and trailer expert, Bobby Fantarella, has these suggestions for making sure the riding season is full of good, safe times. Some of these tips are do-it-yourself. Others need a mechanic.

Most manufacturers recommend service every twelve thousand miles or every twelve months. Since most people will never put twelve thousand miles on it, annual service is cheap insurance.

Basic service consists of: pulling the wheels, re-packing the bearings with fresh grease, and putting new seals back.

One crucial thing people seem to forget is to check the air pressure in all the tires. Low pressure can cause sway, poor tire wear, etc. Also, when putting proper air pressure in tires, don't forget to check the spare, too.

Check that all running lights, blinkers, and brake lights are working.

Check the 'break-away' battery. That little guy engages your brakes if your trailer ever becomes separated from the tow vehicle. To see if the 'break-away' battery is working: While the trailer is properly hooked up, pull the safety key out. Then try to move the vehicle a few feet. If you can feel the brakes working, you're fine. If you don't feel any braking, chances are your battery is shot or you have other wiring problems.

As for the flooring: At least three or four times a year, you should pull the mats out of the trailer. Wash the floor and the bottom of the mats. While the mats are out, inspect the floor. Even aluminum floors can have problems if urine is left to sit between the mats and the floor. If everything is OK, wait until both the mats and the floor are completely dry before putting them back in the trailer.

Lastly: Lubricate your hitch, hinges on doors, ramps, etc. (WD-40, PB Blaster, spray grease, etc.). Give your trailer a good 'once over' checking for any problems: Window trim, screens hanging out, etc.

Take care of your trailer, and it will take care of you, along with its precious cargo.

OUTRUNNING RAIN

I t started out as a lazy Sunday ride. We headed out with Comet and Pep. The sun was high and hot. Nearby fields had just been cleared of first-cut bales.

Down the road, new neighbors were having a keg party of sorts in their front yard. One man pretended to cast from his skiff. It was on grass, not water. Same for him, I imagine. They waved and invited us to join them.

Rufus and Firecracker, two easy-going geldings on the corner, called to our mares. We stopped to let everyone sniff.

After a few miles of gravel road, passing fields and woods, we reached my friend's house. I went inside where to visit while Steve let the horses graze for a spell.

Another mile brought us to the top of a hill where we could see clear to the Eastern Iowa Airport, six miles away. The airport was in the midst of a thunderstorm. We watched as a plane flew into thick clouds before safely landing.

The wind quickened. The sky darkened. Birds quieted. Smells grew intense. The storm was barreling south, heading across the cornfields and directly toward us.

I could hear my mother's words ringing in my ears: Always walk the last mile. Never let them run for the barn.

We asked our horses to move out. On the dirt road and its grassy shoulder, we galloped. Past the cemetery. Past Rufus and Firecracker. Past the lawn party. ("Come back for a cold one!" they shouted.)

We raced those last two miles with the dark, heavy curtain of storm at our heels. We screeched right into the barn, like teenagers into an empty school parking lot. We laughed at the rain as it came down in sheets. And thanked our horses for their fine condition.

PONYING

Mornings, I halter three horses and ride one bareback for the half-mile trek down our road, across a stone wall, across a neighbor's yard, and into the big field where I've taped off two acres with electric fence. Evenings, I return with them.

Now, I'm no wiz, but here's what I've learned: Successful ponying is like successful conference calls or field trips:

- Have a good leader.
- Be organized and follow the itinerary.
- Maintain protocol and etiquette.
- Be patient and bring the slower ones up to speed.

Organization and following the itinerary
After everyone is haltered with lines draped across their withers, I mount up and collect lead lines off their backs (I've found this method preferable to holding reins and three lines while trying to get on Shea, who's about sixteen hands.)

Then we open the gate and walk through it. Then we pick sides, with antagonistic horses separated. Off we go!

Protocol and Etiquette
- No running.
- Everyone moves onto the shoulder when cars pass.
- Wait for the slow poke when crossing the stone wall.
- Everyone goes around the same side of the tree.
- Ponied horses may not lead.
- No switching sides.

Patience with the slower ones

That'd be Trixie. And being a pony, she picks her moments to try my patience. She's slow when she wants to be. She likes to hesitate when we're almost there or almost home. My interpretation? She's hoping I'll drop her line and let her graze just outside the gate.

It's a parade of sorts. When I first started, it was more like a circus. A bad circus with lots of mindless circling, off-balance missteps, and 'who's on first' antics.

One time, I got everyone set and reached for the gate, reached a little more, and fell right off with the four horses all around me and an open gate. Another time, I brought them home in the pitch dark with no flashlight or reflective gear, racing down the road before oncoming cars.

We're getting it down to a routine. Apparently, it's an entertaining routine: My neighbor said he and his wife look forward to their cocktail hour show each evening: watching me assembling the crew and heading off.

ANOTHER PONYING SEASON

The circus is back in town. I've resumed ponying the horses back and forth from my neighbor's field.

This year, I decide to cut through the woods instead of traveling up the road and across my neighbor's yard like I did last year. The decision is due to safety and neighborly concerns. Peppermint is new to ponying, and I don't want to deal with cars, motorbikes, and three horses all at once. And with the ground so wet, we'd trash any nice lawn with a single pass.

We travel down the paved road, down the dirt road, across a trench, down the logging trail, cut through the woods, and into the field. Good days, it takes ten minutes. Bad days, it takes longer.

Bad days: When we're not all on the same page and we need to discuss; when one horse gets loose and we have to lure her back to the team; when horses decide they would rather spend a few more hours at the field. Thank you very much. Come back later when we're ready; when this white girl loses her already limited ability to jump onto a big saddleless horse.

At first, I thought this new, off-road route would be easier. That was before we negotiated The Trench for the first time. The Trench is an innocuous-looking swale next to the dirt road. It drops off the road and is filled with mud and water.

No big deal, right? Spring jitters and horse camaraderie make it a big deal on a few days.

We approach it and Shea refuses. I suggest she reconsider. She LEAPS across it. Shea is half Belgian. Her leaps are not balletic, more like an out-of-shape, drunk guy scrambling over a Jersey barrier.

Thankfully, Brooke and Peppermint follow. Riding bareback and jostling with lead lines, I am just happy to stay on and still have the other horses in hand.

Since they are being drama queens, I suggest we cross again and again until it becomes the trench and not The Trench. We move on. You know when you're moving through an area of mud or snow and you try to step lightly, quickly, even daintily, in the hopes that you can avoid sinking in? Well, my horses seem to do the same thing—they're definitely NOT happy with walking calmly through as they sink into a foot of mud with every step.

Brooke, the boss mare, likes to avoid it altogether. She'll try to swerve way wide and walk through brush. I like a strong-minded horse, just not while ponying. And having a discussion with a horse whilst ponying is like trying giving directions while ordering pizza. Plenty of room for mixed messages.

After the mud gauntlet, we have a stretch of dry woods. We like dry woods, except when one horse goes the wrong way around a tree. I need to keep them close. At this point, they're getting excited. They can see the sunny, green field. They can smell it. They can hear the new spring grass calling.

Hello? Listen to me, please.

The final stretch is across the field. Their fenced-in section is a hundred yards yonder. Why, they seem to ask, can't we graze right here? If one of them drops her head to grab grass, her idea can be downright contagious.

Plus, there can be up to a dozen turkeys milling around the field. Those courting toms can seem bigger than dogs with blue and red heads and puffed out plumage. Spook worthy, for sure.

I hook the halters and bridle on a branch and turn back to watch them now grazing contentedly. It's contentment sharpened by the journey.

A PAUSE

For all the backaches and isolation of working a farm and being self-employed, there'd be plenty of moments missed if I had a "real job."

In this case, a doe and tiny fawn entered the pasture through the side that has wooden, three-rail fencing. They tried to cross over another stretch that's all wire sheep fencing. The doe hopped over. The fawn could not and jogged up and down the fence line, trying to find a way. After some thirty minutes, and with the fawn seeming more and more frantic, the doe hopped back into the pasture, and they both ran back whence they came. It brought to mind a poem, written by my dad, Sam Butcher:

Jumping the Fence

Five strands of barbed wire stretch between
our alfalfa and the willow thicket,
where the fawns are born.
In July, when doe and fawn rush
to safety in the willows,
the doe clears the fence in a bound
while the fawn scoots under
the bottom wire, quick as a cat.
By spring all deer will jump the fence.
Imagine the dance before
the young deer jumps:
the top strand is no longer so high,
but the barbs are very sharp,
and the old way still serves.
Think of the first time
the deer lifts its head,
drives its powerful legs
and never looks back.

SUMMER HORSE TIME

Sure, I cherish all seasons of horse time. But gotta say, these warm summer days I cherish the most. It's relaxed. If you stop and let it, fun stuff happens.

I am sitting out at the barn tonight, as I often do after dinnertime. The horses come and go. Mostly they linger around me. A dog sits at my feet. I spin and inadvertently spill a bit of beer on her back. Peppermint licks it up, like a mama bear. The dog is relaxed enough to stay there and let it happen and even joins her. Dog and pony lapping together.

Summer.

It reminds me of another moment years ago with my rescued thoroughbred, Handsome. It was hot. Real hot. I was wearing shorts and a running bra. I had just hosed him down. He was being fresh, and I should have asked him to give me some space, but let it go.

He muzzled my shoulder and grabbed the shoulder strap of my running bra in his teeth and snapped it.

Summer.

Most horses like going in water, especially when the weather's hot. The process can be a bit like introducing a kid to a healthy food: Hey, this is actually good! In my experience, tt's just a matter of making the outing positive. Getting cool on a hot day—what could be more positive?

My horse, Shea, is part draft, and big horses have a tougher time in the heat. These past few summers, she's been like a golden retriever when it comes to water: Oh, this again? I like this. Go in again? No problem.

We both like going in over our heads. I float on her back, holding onto her mane as a security blanket, and then, I feel her touch bottom again as we get back toward shore. Doesn't get much better than this.

One particular outing, we played with my mom's black lab, Lark. She had no previous experience with horses, and, at first, I think she would have preferred to keep it that way. But when I asked her to play fetch, she seemed to forget about the thousand-pound animal between her and the stick.

HIGH TIMES ON HAY FIELDS

A ll around the northern hemisphere, farmers are putting away gazillions of bales of hay for the winter.

My folks have fond memories of haying season in their home states of Michigan and Ohio. By age ten, they were learning to drive farm trucks on the fields and back roads. They hung out under the tanning sun with siblings and cousins. It was busy, tiring, and fun. It was family and community coming together.

On Maine fields around here, families and friends are still rounded up to get it all done. The whole Bailey gang was on the field when I picked up a hundred bales in Pennellville.

Steve Bailey runs a small beef operation in Durham. He and his wife have three children of their own and another two they adopted when his sister passed away a few years ago.

From ages six to fifteen, they all pull their weight. The older boys, Kaleb and David, load hay and are learning to drive the tractor. Sister Jamie can swing the bales mightily, too. The younger ones, Kohen and Karleigh, drive the truck and trailer as hay is loaded from the field and otherwise do whatever they can.

It was another family affair on a field in Pownal where the Burnhams cut eight hundred bales last week. I swung by to pick up a hundred bales.

Donald Burnham, seventy-eight, has been farming for decades. He beamed and yelled to me from his tractor, "Your horses are going to get fat on this!"

His son, Rob, and nephew, Nick Harriman, stacked bales seven-high onto the hay wagon. They're young and strong. When they joke around, they start throwing bales at each other as if they were beach balls.

Combined, these families will put up over twenty thousand bales. Meanwhile, I got two hundred into my barn.

On the field, my mom drove the truck. Friends Chris Lombard and Ashley Hutchinson helped pack my truck and stock trailer. For the offloading, though, I was on my own.

My three teenage sons were all away at summer jobs. I missed them dearly. That's OK. Nothing a good radio station and cold beverages couldn't solve. It's haying season, after all. And it was only two hundred bales.

RELAX TO LEARN

The line 'Relax to Learn' could sum up my summer. For the first time in years, I devoted whole mornings and afternoons to riding, exploring new terrain, and pushing myself through those mental walls of hesitation and fear.

With a few added skills, I gained more confidence and worked with my horse in a bosal instead of a snaffle bit. (A bosal is a shaped, rawhide noseband, hung by a leather hanger over the horse's poll and attached to mecate reins.) With the change in equipment came greater awareness and greater softness.

The horses, of course, taught me the most. Pep and Comet are different characters, both sensitive in their own ways. Neither likes to stand still. Neither has a lot of tolerance for the nearby firing range. And Pep, in particular, shows a strong distaste for bikes of all kinds.

By summer's end, it was not so much that they'd become desensitized to these things but that I'd gotten better at working with them, predicting reactions, making things better for them.

RELAX TO LEARN, II

This I believe: Pep is a solid, sensitive mare. We have a trusting partnership. We understand each other's subtlest cues. Oftentimes, our minds are one, except when they aren't. A peculiar disconnection crept into an otherwise pleasant Sunday ride. It happened as we descended into a dark, thickly green ravine.

Up to then, the ride had been one of the summer's best. With cooler temperatures and a summer's worth of conditioning, we covered eight miles in no time. We galloped stretches of field, skirted the firing range, and handled crazy cyclists and motorbikes without incident.

The ravine was the only hurdle to clear before the home stretch of gravel road. At its top, Pep came to a dead stop. I pointed her down the path and gave her a second to make the choice. She said, 'No, I'd rather go this way.'

I said, "How about we go this way?"

She said, 'This way is better.'

I said, "We've done this a half dozen times. C'mon."

When horses manage steep descents, most of them hunker down on their butts. When our discussion ended, I shifted my weight, anticipating this downhill scoot. Nuthin' doing. Pep launched herself, like a rocket, off the side of the ravine.

Ever seen a dock dog competition, where dogs hurl themselves off a platform and into a pool? That was us, but without the water.

We landed. I discovered I was still in the saddle. I grabbed Pep's mane, hugged her neck, and we ducked through the undergrowth. She scooted through the briars and hustled up the other side.

We popped onto the road like kids at the end of a playground slide, shook off some leaves, checked for scrapes, and continued toward home.

Whatever happened to a horse's sense of self-preservation?

Whatever happened to 'A Horse Looks after Her Rider?'

None of that. Today's lesson, evidently, was "Relax to Learn."

THREE:

Horsemen & Horsewomen

KYLA POLLARD

Most of today's professional horsemen stepped into that role like they step into their jeans every morning. Born into it and charged with big tasks at a young age, the job comes naturally. While the rest of us were learning how to drive a car, they were learning how to drive cattle. They were staying on colts while we were trying to stay on varsity.

Families like the Blacks and Neuberts, for instance, gave their children fine head starts for carrying on a tradition of exemplary horsemanship. But within this next generation, there's a share of outsiders, too. Through grit and spirit, they've worked their way into the field from a different perspective—not as natural-born talents but as students. Kyla Pollard is one to watch.

"There are very few people as dedicated as Kyla," said friend Jonathan Field, one of Canada's most prominent clinicians. "She's always first there and last to leave. It's like a quest for her...The way Ray Hunt and Tom Dorrance worked, Kyla is a good representative of that way with horses. And she remains humble in the process."

Long-legged and thirty-eight years old, Kyla got her start in the pony clubs of New Brunswick, Canada. By high school, she was trading stall mucking for a chance to ride, exercising horses for others, and learning from a large animal vet.

After graduating from the University of New Brunswick and the Maritime Forest Ranger School, Pollard interviewed for forestry positions. It came down to two job offers: one in Maine, one in British Columbia. Same job, same pay. She couldn't decide.

The Canadian interviewer phoned the young candidate from his home. He was sitting on his patio, trying to convince her to head west. His horses called out and Kyla heard them. The conversation switched to this shared 'hobby' (as stated on her resume). She took the job.

Settling into a new life in Fort Saint James, B.C. (about five hundred miles north of Vancouver and five hundred miles west of Edmonton), Pollard finally acquired a horse of her own, a Morgan-Arabian gelding with plenty of go. Too much go.

"He'd take off on me," said Pollard, who resisted the advice to move to a bigger bit and discovered Pat Parelli's program and the methods we generally call 'natural horsemanship.' "I dug in and learned everything I could," she said.

It didn't take long for Pollard to gravitate toward Ray Hunt. She audited his course at the Gang Ranch, which hosted him annually for many years, and loved what she saw.

Pollard was scrambling together funds to return and participate in the next Hunt clinic there when she learned of his passing. It was a wake-up call, she said. "Ray's death was a big turning point for me. It made me realize these guys don't live forever. From that point on, I vowed to ride as much as possible with his and Tom Dorrance's best students."

At this point, said Pollard, horses became "a major focus and push for basically every decision I made in life." She started saving money and vacation days for further education.

The next pivot point came at the Mane Event in Chilliwack, B.C., where Martin Black was starting a colt in the three-day Trainers Challenge. "I was enthralled. You could not keep me away from that round pen," recalled Pollard.

A few weeks later, Pollard booked a plane ticket and was on her way to Black's colt starting school in Texas for two months. "I thought I had a really good handle on my horsemanship, a high sensitivity," said Pollard with a laugh. "I so did not. Martin showed me a whole different level of acknowledging where the horse is coming from and how you can make it better for the horse."

Over several years, Pollard worked closely with Black and followed his advice to ride as many horses as she could. In short order, Pollard has ridden or started nearly four hundred horses and has acquired fans on both ends of Canada.

Heather Touchie is one of them. She rescued a yearling from a notorious New Brunswick neglect case involving dozens of dead and starving horses. She wasn't sure how he'd be under saddle, given the gelding's "horrible start," said the horsewoman.

Kyla agreed to work with him and was "absolutely excellent," said Touchie. "She instilled a lot of confidence in him through her work. Kyla was very aware that this horse would need to be mentally ready for whatever job he'd have. She set him up for success."

Pollard likes to set students up for success, too. Often, she'll lecture and present theoretical matters before heading out to the arena. "I like to prepare them mentally so that when we do get to ride, they understand," said Pollard. "You can set the tone for the class by providing a theory lecture."

Among today's horsemen and women, Pollard sets herself apart by her willingness to put herself in the student's saddle, sometimes literally. "That's a big difference I really liked with her," said client Jocelyne Noel. "She'll jump on the horse and see what you're dealing with. She'll correct it in the horse and then help you correct what you're doing. That's helped a lot."

For Pollard: Once a student, always a student.

This fall, she worked for Golden Bear Outfitting, an elite outfitting company in northwest B.C. She led a pack of five horses over miles of remote, challenging terrain. Her boss had a good chuckle when Pollard told them she didn't own a gun or know-how to fire one. It being bear country and all, she picked up that skill too.

"I've been there. I find myself not being critical, just accepting the fact that everyone starts somewhere. Maybe their whole life, they used the horse as a tool. Like a motor bike. Then the person starts to have some awareness of where the horse is coming from. They didn't realize it. So, I'm very empathetic to people's learning experience," she said.

Her life as a student, once considered a handicap, might just be her finest asset.

Back in B.C., Valarie Crowley has watched Pollard work with Crowley's daughter, Willa. "She responds to the needs of the student, the mood of the horse," said Crowley. "The most beautiful part of Kyla's instruction is the respect and love that she has for her horses. Willa knows that she is not just learning to ride a horse. She is learning how to develop a relationship with a horse, and through this relationship, earning the right to ride."

THE HORSE-HUMAN TOUCH

I was talking with Chris Lombard the other day about horsemanship. The dictionary calls it the 'skill of riding horses.'

But we know it as the relationship with the horse and the skills around that relationship. "It's not only how to handle horses," said Lombard, "but how to be around them."

So often, he said, we can get caught up in "This guy says this. That guy says that. Who do you believe?" It can be an exhausting search for answers in all the wrong places.

The thing that really matters, he said, is not your connection to a trainer. It's your connection to your horse. When Lombard works with horses, he's giving them something that'll last a lifetime. Sounds high-minded, but we all do it.

Treatment—good or bad—can be as indelible as a tattoo. Just ask anyone with a rescued horse or one with a troubled past. Treatment sticks.

Kyla Pollard knows this from starting scores of colts in New Brunswick and British Columbia, Canada. "The different way you work through the process will create a different horse," said Pollard, who has worked with Martin Black and Jonathan Field.

Recently, Lombard met horses who'd spent time with Kris and Nik Kokal, the New Hampshire brothers whose impressive horsemanship was highlighted in the mustang documentary, *Wild Horse, Wild Ride*. How did he know they'd been with the Kokals? "I could feel it," he said.

As we look ahead to the riding season, perhaps the best strategy is not to register for the next great clinic, but to pause for a moment and look in. "Believe yourself," suggested Lombard. "People have gone clinician crazy instead of thinking for themselves. You have to get back to feeling it on the inside." Then perhaps find the talented horseman or woman who can help improve your partnership and your communication.

I KNEW YOU BY YOUR COW HANDLING

You and I might see a connection between family members or close friends by the way they walk or talk. But by the way they sort cattle??

That's the way my friend, Elijah Moore, connected the dots with Martin Black. Moore was watching Black at a recent clinic in New Hampshire. Something about the way he worked the cows reminded Moore of his old friend, Newt Wright.

Wright was born in Montana in 1935 and lived in Idaho, Oregon, and Arizona (where he and Moore became close). He was admired by many as an intellectual horseman. He was a man who spent a lot of time thinking about how horses think, how cows think, how dogs think.

Wright taught farriers, taught riders, taught bull riders. And he was a constant student, always wanting to learn more, according to memorials left on his website. He died suddenly last year in Bozeman, Montana.

Moore asked Black about his cattle work. And did he know a fellow by the name of Newt Wright? "Martin laughed and said Newt could handle a herd of cattle better than anyone I've ever seen," recalled Moore.

Black credited Wright for teaching him some excellent and essential cow-handling skills back when he was younger.

Incredible, isn't it, how a subtle yet signature technique, handed down from one cowboy to another can connect dots and paint a picture? Such a picture many of us would never see.

TERRY MCCLARE

When I adopted Brooke, I knew I'd be challenged. No regrets. I've learned a lot in the process—about my own skills (or lack thereof) and about the need for assertiveness.

There were kinks in our rapport. Never was that more apparent than at a recent Chris Lombard clinic:

We had had an uneventful morning of ground work and an hour of walking, trotting, backing, confronting 'scary' obstacles, and so on. But then, when I asked her to canter, she tossed me.

I wanted to address our issues right away and the right way. I called Terry McClare, hooked up the trailer, and headed to Footloose Farm in Brownfield, Maine. Footloose Farm is home to about thirty horses. McClare trains, teaches lessons, and hold clinics about once a month. McClare grew up riding. She did just about everything, from 4H and gaming to dressage and jumping.

In 1990 at the age of twenty-eight, she went to her first Buck Brannaman clinic. She's attended one or more of his clinics every year since then and has traveled to Brannaman's Wyoming ranch to start colts. "It makes sense to me because it makes sense to the horse," said McClare of Brannaman's methods.

I brought Brooke into a small indoor arena at Footloose Farm and handed the lead line to Terry. Right away, she noticed Brooke's braciness. She was flexing laterally alright, but her feet were still planted. I began to understand that what I'd been asking Brooke to do was more mechanical than through feel. She might have been yielding her head, but the rest of the body wasn't into it. She was getting away with poor form because I didn't know any better.

Terry got to work. She showed me several exercises to help Brooke understand how to move her feet without coming unglued. She showed me how to ask for a true bend, not a cagey one.

Groundwork is really helpful for a horse like Brooke, she told me. We can ask her to bend, remind her how to move her feet, work through transitions on the ground, and set ourselves up for better in-saddle work.

Repeated trot-to-canter transitions on the ground were especially helpful. Terry taught me how to ask for them without nagging.

Being away from her buddies, scary tarps and tractors, high energy environments—these are all issues for Brooke. "When something bothers her, put her to work," said Terry. "Then she'll settle."

She showed me how to be pro-active (again, without nagging) in the saddle, too.

The best advice involved our dreaded trot-to-canter transition—the source of bucks and my own injury-induced anxiety. Terry taught me to approach it from a more relaxed and patient position. I learned that, for now, we could approach a canter almost by accident, to trot, trot, trot until moving to a canter simply becomes the easy alternative.

After Brooke's two weeks at Footloose Farm and my three trips there to work with her, I loaded up the trailer with a smile on my face. We hadn't smoothed things out entirely, but we had a great new start.

"Coming out of this, you will have more tools to show her that she can get out of trouble or scary situations," said McClare, as we assessed the progress.

We talked about moving forward to new challenges. "Sometimes you have to stay this side of trouble," she said. "Sometimes you have to go to the other side and work through it. Otherwise, it'll be worse the next time."

GREG ELIEL

G reg Eliel's recent clinic in Durham, Maine, was the fourth visit for this Wisdom, Montana, man, who's worked with Buck Brannaman and developed horse-related programs for executive leadership.

Like so many clinicians, Eliel spends months on the road. I asked him about the touring and he answered candidly: "It's demanding. You invest a lot in these horses and in these people. To come back, see the changes and the successes—that's the paycheck."

Michelle Richardson of Harpswell has participated in several Eliel clinics. One year, she brought her "wild and crazy" Tennessee Walker. After four days, she had a different horse, she said. "He teaches you to listen, to work with softness," said Richardson. "He'll stop and explain things without making you feel like an idiot."

Indeed, Eliel related easily to the participants, recalling his earlier days, working with his father on the family ranch. "What I lacked in timing and feel, I made up for in quantity. You're where I was then. My horses didn't always have softness. But they figured it out in spite of me. They got pretty good because they had jobs."

He worked with Tamara Gutierrez and her Morgan from Phippsburg. "At the end of the journey, we'll both be more confident," said Gutierrez. "That's what we need."

I asked Eliel about his new program involving corporate types. He said the same principles that work with horses, work with people. "Horse work is all about leadership. In the corporate world, mid- and upper management is used to leading by pressure. Pressure doesn't get it done. But release of pressure gets it done. You can't move a fourteen-hundred-pound animal with pressure. These clients see how pure and simple it can be."

BRYAN NEUBERT

Neubert is one of the few people who worked with the three men many consider to be the founders of natural horsemanship: Ray Hunt, Bill and Tom Dorrance.

To hear him tell it, Neubert just lucked out. He happened to find work with Ray Hunt and happened to live next door to Tom Dorrance.

"In hindsight, I was extremely blessed. I could not have been in a better place anywhere," said Neubert, who now travels widely as a clinician.

Hunt and Dorrance both considered clinics an unrewarding occupation, recalled Neubert. It's a sentiment he sometimes shares. "Occasionally someone takes it and runs with it. If you find one person in the bunch who wants to learn, that'll be a success," said Neubert. "People think a clinic is the answer, that it's going to turn the light on," continued Neubert. "But it depends on what you do with it."

Neubert tells his students to assume they're not going to make progress during the clinic. "It's going to be at home that it happens, after you start practicing," he said.

Bryan traveled with Tom Dorrance as he started to offer clinics in the 1970s. Back then, holding clinics was a brand new idea. "I thought the word 'clinic' had something to do with a hospital," said Neubert with a laugh. And yes, he confirmed, he has never turned on a computer. Ever. He'll take intuition over Internet anytime.

Neubert said Dorrance told his students, "Don't try too hard because it'll keep you from getting it."

Neubert sees this in his students, too. "If I'm asking a second grader, 'what's nine plus nine?' and I tell him 'I'm going to whack you if you don't know the answer,' that's not conducive to learning. If people are calm, they'll get it...Cool it. Let it happen."

ELIJAH MOORE

"Between the two of us, we can fix just about anything that has to do with a horse." That's what horseman Elijah Moore likes to say. The two—Moore and his wife of thirty years, veterinarian Cynthia Reynolds, are an accomplished pair. Reynolds is well known for her work with acupuncture and chiropractic treatments on horses.

Moore particularly likes to work with troubled horses, or shall we say troubled riders with their horses. He's started and trained thousands of horses, worked as a farrier, worked on the family ranch, worked with vets, just about done it all. "But I just keep learning," he told me.

Moore comes from a long line of well-respected cowboys in southern Utah. His grandfather, Elijah Moore, rode until he was ninety-four and is a legend in those parts.

In Utah historical archives, the elder Moore's name comes up with the likes of Butch Cassidy. That Moore wasn't an outlaw but a successful rancher and horseman. In the first half of the 1900s, he was a Texas Ranger and one of the first cattlemen to move herds into southern Utah. "I grew up around good cowboys," the younger Moore told me.

The grandson certainly didn't fall far from the tree; he's old school. "He was born a hundred years too late," said Reynolds with a laugh.

The couple first moved to Maine in 1986 when Reynolds got her first veterinarian job in Belfast. Since then, they have traveled west and then back to Searsport again as work and interests moved them.

I visited Moore at his Searsport farm to listen and learn. I also wanted to show my girls some cows before next month's ranch clinic with Martin Black. Moore helped me with some initial roping skills, too.

He and Reynolds have seven horses, cows, sheep, chickens, and dogs at the Flying M in Searsport. There are nicely outfitted indoor and outdoor arenas, trails, paddocks, and pens.

I asked Moore about groundwork. Some trainers love it. Some don't. Some riders always start work on the ground. Some don't have a clue. I found his answer compelling: "Groundwork makes the rider softer," he told me. "It makes you understand the horse better. Also, something changes with the horse when you work him on the ground."

We worked in the arena. His horse was a lively Arabian yet he stayed ground-tied for an hour while Moore instructed me. But later, when ridden, the gelding was as light as could be. Wow!

Moore doesn't call himself a clinician. He prefers one-on-one work. I do, too. I just wished I had had a tape recorder to catch every word.

KATHLEEN THRELFALL

Many of us know a little something about trailblazing in a man's world. Starting out, I worked in the *Providence Journal*'s large sports department—all men. Then I moved to another newspaper with an all-male sports department. You learn to pursue your passions, barriers, and judgments notwithstanding.

Kathleen Threlfall is doing just that with her new leatherwork business in British Columbia, Canada. At age twenty-four, she's showing how a savvy cowgirl can excel in the male-dominated world of saddle work.

Two years ago, Threlfall began an apprenticeship with renowned saddle maker Don Loewen in Merritt, B. C. She started making leggings and advanced into saddle work.

"She's very good, very attentive," said Loewen, who was honored this year with the Joe Marten Memorial Award for the Preservation of Cowboy Heritage in British Columbia. "She knew what she wanted and worked pretty hard at it."

Breaking into the saddle-making business can be challenging:

- There's the equipment, costing about $5,000 and including a good sewing machine, hand tools, stamps, and a marble work piece.
- There's the fierce competition.
- There's the cost of maintaining an inventory.

Threlfall started wisely and modestly by focusing on chaps, armitas, chinks, and other leatherware. She works out of Loewen's Merritt shop, maintains a website, and takes her goods to trade shows.

As wearers will attest, the key to leggings is in the fit. Threlfall makes a pattern for every pair. The result is happy customers.

"She's mastered pattern fitting," said Loewen.

Rancher Tim Thomas likes his armitas so much, he's hardly worn them. He discovered Threlfall's work at the Mane Event, a major horse expo in Chilliwack, B.C. While there, he had his measurements taken and ordered a pair. "They're beautiful. I don't want to get them dirty," he laughed.

Thomas runs a large cattle ranch in British Columbia's interior and stays busy with twelve hundred head of cattle. He said he has about six pairs of leggings. "But these fit way better than my others."

For Threlfall, the leatherwork is part of a bigger passion that includes horse care and horsemanship. She's worked with Jonathan Field and Stefanie Travers and recently moved to a small ranch in Merritt where she looks after seven horses.

While her biggest customer pool is of local, working cowboys, she's shipped her wares to elsewhere in Canada, the U.S., and Europe.

Her goal is to develop her own line of gear, including saddles. As she progresses, she learns and incorporates new ideas into her products.

Established saddle makers, like Loewen, she said, "produce artwork...based on a lifetime of work. I'd love to produce leatherwork of that caliber. It just takes time."

Her commitment to the Western lifestyle hasn't gone unnoticed. "It's really good to see a gal like that interested and dedicated...not just in leatherwork but in horsemanship," said Thomas. "Young people don't necessarily follow their passions, but she does. She's going to be something."

RANDY RIEMAN

There are good horsemen out there. They're good to their horses and can handle whatever comes their way. Horses and humans alike join up and follow them.

There are good horse minds, too. They come up with the perfect way to express what we riders feel but struggle to say or write about our horses, our journeys, and our partnerships. And then there are good horse ambassadors. They share the message and make us feel good about time spent with horses. They remind us to cherish and they welcome non-horse folk into the fold.

Finding all these traits in one person is rare. But you'll find them in Randy Rieman. I first heard about Rieman from a friend heading out to the two-thousand-three-hundred-acre Pioneer Mountain Ranch in Dillon, Montana. There, Reiman runs a horsemanship school where riders can stay in cabins and get one-on-one schooling.

Rieman, a protégé of Bill Dorrance, first evaluates each new student. "We talk a lot about why they're here. I watch them ride. I'm going to see if I can spot something, some misunderstanding. Then I might start making suggestions."

Perhaps his key horsemanship tenet is "To have the horse move toward freedom, not move away from pressure."

He believes that if you're not expanding your horse's comfort zone, you're shrinking it. Ideally, a rider needs to provide a "constant challenge to go beyond what the horse knows." That's why he likes to take clients out of the arena. From his ranch, "We leave like we're late and come home like we don't care if we ever get there."

The ranch sits next to 3.3 million acres of the Beaverhead National Forest. Those expanding comfort zones will include encounters with antelope, grouse, snakes, and more. "You can trot for ten miles and never look back," said Rieman.

Rieman has started thousands of colts and ridden thousands of miles. For nine years, he worked at the Parker Ranch on Hawaii's Big Island, one of the oldest and biggest ranches in the country.

He works with colts and with older "rehab" horses "to get them more gentle, more handy, more usable in more situations," he said.

After long stays there and in Nevada, California, and New Mexico, he made his way back to Montana five years ago. Along the way, he acquired a love and talent for reading and writing cowboy poetry. The *San Francisco Chronicle* called Rieman "the hypnotic master of cowboy poetry."

Cowboy poetry is rhymed, metered verse written by someone who has lived a significant portion of his or her life in cattle country. "The verse reflects an intimate knowledge of that way of life, and the community from which it maintains itself in tradition," according to the National Endowment of the Arts.

Rieman has performed at the annual National Cowboy Poetry Gathering in Elko, Nevada, for over two decades, including as guest of honor. The Gathering is "the nation's greatest celebration of the American West, its people, culture and traditions," according to the Western Folklife Center. This year it features nearly fifty poets, musicians, and musical groups from the United States, Canada, and Australia, performing on seven stages at four different venues.

Indeed, talking with Rieman or listening to one of his recitations gives you the feel of a sunny ride in open country when the rhythm of your horse and the specialness of the moment bring a lasting smile to your face.

Randy Rieman – Sidebar

Aside from his talents as a poet, poet reciter, and rawhide braider, Rieman is also a talented horseman. He has traveled from his home in Montana for clinics in Minnesota and Michigan. Sponsors and participants reflected on their experiences:

Kathy Mueller runs Equitation Station, a facility outside of Minneapolis. She hosted Rieman for several days. "I really appreciated his authenticity, knowledge, great stories, willingness to work with the people and horses right where they were at, and help them improve.

"I have mostly a dressage barn, and his methods and understanding of the horse-human relationship were right in line with what I like to teach. Plus, he added some new dimensions to our work with tarps, flags, and group patterns."

Jill Manske adds, "I wasn't quite sure what to expect from this 'cowboy clinic.' I'm certain that Randy wasn't quite sure what to expect from us either! It was quite a sight—women in breeches and boots, riding around a lanky guy in the cowboy hat. Well, that guy in the cowboy hat certainly gave us our money's worth....It was immediately apparent that Randy was all about the horse, about laying the foundation for good riding and for a good horse/rider partnership.

"I was surprised by how much of his approach and focus was on precisely things that are the foundations of dressage—suppleness, transitions, bend, bringing the hind leg under the horse, riding the back (not the head!).

"He is a gifted communicator—to both human and equine. He focused on getting our horses to pay attention to us, to respond to the lightest aids. However, he also helped us demand more from our horses and helped us communicate more clearly and effectively. Some of his oft-repeated phrases were:

- Take the horse before the horse takes you.
- If it isn't working for you, try something else.

"In the middle of working on something, he will go off on a story. Pretty soon, I figured out that these stories had a purpose. Not only were they a means of getting a point across, but when he paused to talk, it allowed the riders to 'get out of their heads' a bit (since we sometimes overthink things). It also gave time for the horses to figure something out."

TOMAS GIMENEZ

We'd all like to improve the lives of horses. For most of us, that means making sure our own horses are well cared for and safe. Once in a while, we can reach out and do right for other horses too.

Dr. Tomas Gimenez has inarguably improved the lives of thousands of horses. And thanks to him, thousands of future horses will survive and thrive too.

Dr. Gimenez retired recently from his position as primary instructor at Technical Large Animal Emergency Rescue, Inc. (TLAER), an operation he founded seventeen years ago with his now ex-wife Dr. Rebecca Gimenez.

Originally from Mexico, Gimenez studied in Sweden and Germany before rising as a professor emeritus at Clemson University in South Carolina.

He has a keen, quiet sense of humor, loves having exactly the right tool for the job, and is passionate and animated about saving large animals in disaster situations.

Those interests in horses and gadgetry helped fuel a wealth of innovations in the large animal rescue field. Horse stuck in mud? Tangled in brush? Fallen through bridge and into swift water? Trapped in an interstate highway rollover?

If responders to these scenarios had just the right equipment, chances are Dr. Gimenez developed it. If the responders didn't have the right equipment but still rescued the horses quickly, efficiently, and safely, Dr. Gimenez had a hand in training them.

Not all of his equipment was technical. Gimenez once protected a horse's eye with a bra.

I took two TLAER courses. I learned it's pretty easy to kill a horse with a bad rescue attempt. It's pretty easy to get hurt in the process too.

One of the most significant aspects of his legacy is getting large animal rescue legitimate. Fewer imperiled horses will have to rely on a bunch of Good Samaritans trying to jerry-rig a rescue. And fewer horses will die because the firemen didn't know squat about equine behavior.

It's now a heavy rescue specialty, a field which has grown to "encompass global training efforts and recommended equipment for disaster and emergency preparedness, prevention and response," said a recent TLAER press release.

TLAER methods, procedures, and equipment recommendations are now embraced as standards promulgated by the National Fire Protection Association.

Gimenez's last public training was December 7-9, 2012 at the brand new International TLAER Training Facility in Gray, Georgia.

Thanks, Tomas, for the passion, commitment, and ingenuity you brought to the horse world. You've made it a better place.

WOODS KING

My grandfather never lived to be a grandfather. He died when my mother was just twelve. But he left behind memories of fine horse-related accomplishments and a legacy of the love of riding.

I remember stories of my grandfather, Woods King, on each Memorial Day. Most of the stories don't have to do with his military service but of the fun he'd have with his horses and the care he took of them. I think he managed to pass those ideas down a few generations.

Photos from a 1930s album show him riding double as a knight with his real life bride-to-be (my Grannie), Louise Baldwin. He's seen riding three horses standing up, with one foot on each outside horse while the third trots dutifully underneath him.

He was a pivotal member of the oldest mounted police unit in the country, the Cleveland Mounted Police. Before World War II, it was an Ohio National Guard unit. Then it was absorbed into the U.S. Army as the 107th Cavalry Regiment, which he led.

The Cleveland Mounties have paraded in presidential inaugurations in Washington, D.C., won a mounted unit world championship in Chicago, and represented the United States in an international competition in Mexico City.

In 1989 the Cleveland Mounted Police was the only mounted police unit invited to march in the inaugural parade of George H.W. Bush after the parade committee ranked it No. 1 in the country.

My grandfather left the army as a brigadier general and was discharged with a heart condition in 1946. As my mom put it: "He came home from the war and died."

While I feel far removed from the society in which he moved, I nonetheless feel connected through our beloved partners in work and play.

Rest in Peace. Your love of horses lives on.

∂ – ∂

Since writing the feature on my grandfather, Woods King, I have been lucky to hear from some far-flung connections. Tom Devine, a retiree in Colorado, read the article and had this to add, "I met many who served under your grandfather in WWII. They told me: 'He was a man's soldier.' They went on and on about what a great leader he was, how he earned the respect of those who served under him.

Tears would come down many of their cheeks. They said he was the greatest officer they'd ever served under. A man's man."

Another bit of history came to my desk, adding to his involvement with the Cleveland Mounted Police and Troop A of the 107th Ohio Calvary. In 1926 all the police horses fell ill right before Memorial Day, so King and his brother lent the department twenty-two horses from their own stables for the annual Cleveland parade, an effort that earned them special accolades from the city. Later, after King had commanded the 107th and served extensively in China (twice awarded the Legion of Merit), the mounted unit stables would be named after King.

But the most exciting development came from a collector in Dillon, Montana. He had the holster issued to my grandfather. Made by Abercrombie & Fitch, the army issued it to generals exclusively. Patton wore a similar rig to hold the standard issued .45 automatic pistol. It comes with a Sam Browne belt and shoulder strap.

It will be hard to fact-check, but I'm suspending my skepticism for the chance to connect tangibly with the man I never knew. I acquired the rig and the lore to go with it.

HORSE-DRAWN POTATOES

These spuds tasted better. That's what I was thinking as my guests and I polished off plates of delicious Shepody potatoes the other night. The baked skins were thin and crispy. The insides were light, fluffy, and slipped right down with butter, salt, and pepper.

Just a few hours earlier, they'd been harvested in Mechanic Falls, Maine, by a pair of Percheron mares and a hard-working group from the Farmers Draft Horse Mule and Pony Club. The harvest was a culmination of efforts for the twenty-five-year-old club this season.

Accordingly to Steve Akeley, a club director, the group planted about two thousand pounds of seed this spring. (Horses were used then too.) They expected to yield about ten thousand pounds of Kennebec, Shepody, and Russet potatoes, planted over an acre on a backfield of Harvest Hill Farm (also known as Pumpkinland).

Not a lot of folks harvest potatoes with horses lately. In fact, the equipment pulled behind Kenny Robbins's beautiful pair of Percherons was over a hundred years old.

You just don't find potato diggers for draft horse pulling on eBay or craigslist. Trust me; the guys in the Farmers Draft Horse Mule and Pony Club have looked.

On this warm and sunny day, the horses got a good workout as they turned up row after row of big yellow spuds. Robbins, who lives in Canton, conditioned them by driving a flat load behind them to build up their legs and lungs. The girls would pull for 150 feet, and then pause calmly as workers adjusted equipment. Then they'd move out again. Within thirty minutes, hundreds of pounds of potatoes sat dirty but golden on a trailer bed.

After some time, former club president Bill Winslow stepped in with his pair of Belgians. Several other pairs waited their turn and stood quietly tied to trailers, grazing on hay.

Maine has a rich history of potato production, especially in Aroostock County, which, at nearly seven thousand square miles, is the largest American county east of the Mississippi. Kids still get out of school to help with the harvest. Akeley, who is also an equine dentist, remembers it well from his childhood in Mapleton, outside of Presque Isle. He even used his potato-pickin' basket from the old days.

The Farmers Draft Horse Mule and Pony Club claims about two hundred members from all across the country.

THE MEN OF THE HORSEMEN'S RE-UNION

S ome quick impressions of the horsemen at the Horsemen's Re-Union, a new colt-starting event in Paso Robles, California:

"I'm old and I'm chicken." That's what Pat Parelli told emcee Larry Mahan and hundreds of spectators when asked why he wasn't starting his own colts like everyone else. He had his apprentice do it. Parelli ducked out of a lot of the work but didn't mind putting himself in front of the camera as often as possible. Gotta give him credit, though, Parelli held his own in the after-hours events (roping and branding) and withstood the emcees' ribbing with a smile.

Clayton Anderson, protégé of Chris Cox, was smooth and calm. One of my favorite images was on Day Four when everyone moved outdoors to the huge main fairgrounds arena. Anderson worked with his beautiful young filly for an hour on the ground and in the saddle. Then he took off all the gear and just hung out, relaxing by draping his tall frame over her back. She stood there, licking her lips and watching the controlled chaos around them. When he took off her rope halter and moved away, she followed.

This was the same filly that reminded him of a wild horse when emcee Russell Dilday asked about her on Day Two. "She's sensitive, like a mustang," said Anderson. "Their awareness is a lot greater than domestic horses. So more time is necessary and more reinforcement is necessary."

Jim and Luke Neubert, sons of Bryan Neubert, are polite, good-lookin', and fantastic horsemen. The week must have been a welcome pause for them as they're accustomed to traveling from ranch to ranch, starting scores of colts. They had only two apiece, but their no-nonsense, time's-a-wastin' approach showed through all the same.

By Day Four, Luke was sacking out his colt. Oh, but this was extreme sacking out: Pulling a heavy sack behind and in front of his horse in an arena full of young horses, a few cows, barrels, and assorted obstacles. The horse took a while to figure out that the bundle pursuing him didn't want to eat him. We saw Luke galloping whilst flipping the rope from one side to the other as the horse dashed and skittered. When the horse let himself get a good look at the sack, Luke just let him set for a while. After the recess, the pair trotted along the perimeter, pulling the sack like a toddler might drag his baby blanket. No big deal.

Ron Wall: First there's his hat. Fellow Australian, Ken May, who, by the way, was the only horseman with a female apprentice. (Kudos, Ken!) jokingly told me it belonged to Wall's mother, and she had passed it on to Ron. It's dirty, misshaped, unconventional.

Then there's the rest of his get-up: Wall doesn't wear chinks or chaps. And his boots look like Wallabies or maybe old school Timberlands. Sometimes his jeans catch on the top of them. Sometimes they don't. He makes no secret of his self-described 'filthy habits' of smoking and having a few pops. But when it came to horsemanship, the man was one of the most impressive I've ever seen.

Typically, Wall likes to lay down a horse on Day Two. He does so with patience and grace. The horses I saw him work with never seemed panicked or overly-stressed.

Martin Black was asked when he knows laying down has been a good experience for the horse. "When he looks around, sticks one of his front feet forward and then the other and takes his time getting up," he said.

That's what happened with Wall's horses. There was a peaceful, Zen-like flow to all of Wall's sessions. He never moved suddenly. He rarely if ever made eye contact with his horses. He always let them find the answers on their own.

Craig Cameron, like Parelli, withstood a lot of 'old man' and 'this is live, not televised' jokes and seemed to really enjoy the week. He had lots of nice things to say about the event and reflected over coffee one morning. "It's just a great atmosphere. We're not here just to visit. We're here to work. But we get to visit each other and have a good time. They always say with horsemen, if you can't laugh at each other and with each other, what's the point anyway? We're getting out there and having just a really good time. That's important.

"It's a cowboy brotherhood really. I think you have the truest disciples of great horsemanship here. These are guys that are really active in the business, taking it to the public, and showing them really the best way to handle horses."

Now, if only the event would involve rescued horses in lieu of bred horses, I'd be a fan for life!

Horsemen's Re-Union – Sidebar I

Ever watch a good cook in the kitchen? There are often no cookbooks or measuring cups. Experience, intuition, and creativity rule. And so it is with good horsemen and women. They flow with their horses, operating on a level they often find hard to explain. They rely on cues they see easily, react to instinctively but struggle to describe to others. Until now.

Steve Peters delivered a list of ingredients and recipes of sorts to a large gathering of expert horsemen here. In an hour-long presentation of Evidence-Based Horsemanship, a model he developed with Martin Black, Peters described the horse's brain development and function from foal to adult horse. He guided the audience through detailed descriptions of how it learns and matures in the hands of a good trainer. Or otherwise.

For instance, the horse doesn't discriminate between good and bad learning. "But if it feels good, then they'll come back looking for that same experience the next time," said Black, who joined in the question-and-answer session after Peters's presentation.

Trainers Bryan Neubert, Ken May, Pat Parelli, Craig Cameron, and others had questions for Peters after his lecture. Perhaps the most inquisitive among them was Larry Mahan, who had held the title of World Rodeo Champion for five consecutive years and was the subject *The Great American Cowboy*, an Oscar-winning documentary.

He praised the collaboration, "It is pure genius on the part of Martin and Dr. Peters to put together this book. It really opens up a whole new can of worms."

Tom Saunders, a sixth generation Texas horseman, praised Peters as well. "It's something we were seeing but we lacked the vernacular for it."

Many listeners picked up concepts quickly and related them to what they have seen in their own horse work. Peters took time to describe the increased learning potential when horses are given time to dwell and relax after an exercise.

The next morning, Bryan Neubert told a story about giving his horse a break before returning to something challenging. "Why do you think the horse needed that recess?" asked Mahan. "Well, if you'd listened to the doctor's presentation last night, you'd know!" laughed Neubert.

As learning creatures, Peters suggested horses can perform best when in a natural environment, i.e., with ample, varied turnout and with other horses. When asked about working with mustangs versus domestic horses, Peters told the audience, "You have a super bright student in the mustang. You just have to learn to communicate with it. You will succeed if you can get past the sympathetic nervous system, the reactive part of the training."

Participant Clayton Anderson reiterated this point, "A mustang's awareness is a lot greater than a domestic horse's. So, more time is necessary and more reinforcement is necessary."

One attendee described her work with Bureau of Land Management mustangs and added, "Mustangs have dendrites coming out the wazoo! I don't think any learning environment can substitute for a feral herd."

Experts and spectators seemed to agree that Evidence-Based Horsemanship provided a much-needed 'missing link' between science and the sometimes-mysterious art of horse training. "It's so nice that science is backing up what these horsemen are doing," observed one woman. "It's great to see the dovetailing."

The proof was already in the pudding. Now we know the ingredients.

Horsemen's Re-Union – Sidebar II

It'd be easy to come home from an event like the Horsemen's Re-Union completely humbled and downtrodden. After watching nothing-short-of-amazing stuff all week, I was thinking: I know nothing. Even if I win the lottery, quit my job, and devote my life to horsemanship, I'll never learn all I need to learn. That might be true in part. But I'm choosing rose-tinted glasses this time around.

I returned from California and saddled up for a brisk ride in the mud and under grey skies. I was my usual disheveled self, mismatched clothes, and Jed Clampett hat. This time, though, I dressed with pride, knowing that Ron Wall, in my mind the event's most talented trainer, was my equal when it came to appearance.

Peppermint and I moved through the fields, crossed ditches and streams, and finally moved out on drier ground. It wasn't pretty, but I stayed on and had fun. Pep seemed to relish the afternoon as much as I did, responding to my every request quickly and willingly.

Could I be lighter with my cues than I was on the last ride? Could we open and close gates more smoothly today? I think so.

I recalled a visit from a friend two weeks back. He'd never ridden but wanted to try. We put him up on Shea, the gentle giant. He gripped the horn and smiled nervously. He listened attentively to the new foreign language of horse-speak: Try not to grab the reins or pull on her mouth. If you feel you need to stop, just pull one rein to get control of her head and turn her. If you get going too fast, do not clamp down with your legs; that means go faster to her, etc.

After thirty minutes, he dismounted, a little thrilled and a little overwhelmed, just like I had been at the Re-Union. For him, it was the first of what we hope will be many rides as he discovers what most of us already know: We're lucky to be forever learning, forever privileged with the partnership that is riding and horsemanship.

TEMPLE GRANDIN – STRAIGHT TALK

Maybe it's her autism. Maybe it's from growing up with animals. Either way, Temple Grandin is a refreshingly straight talker.

In working with slaughter plants, Grandin has transformed the handling of cattle and other animals. Humane treatment is prioritized and monitored at a whole new level, thanks to her. Gone are such ineffective, nebulous terms as 'properly,' 'adequate,' 'sufficient,' and 'undue pain and suffering.' "What does that mean?" she asked rhetorically.

Instead, as a result of her research and lobbying, plants and handlers are scored on the percentage of animals that run, fall, vocalize, and move by a electric prod. "The things I do are going to make the world a better place," she said. "I get excited about real change in the real world."

The biggest selling point? Research shows good stockmanship pays. Everyone wins when animals are stressed as little as possible. Or, as a farmer in the audience noted of Grandin's methods, "It's not only more humane, more efficient, and less stressful. It's more profitable."

Highlights of her talk:

- Animals worry whenever there is a change in the floor—dirt to metal, metal to concrete, shadow to reflection. Give the animal a chance to put its head down and look.

- When animals are calm, they will stop and look at things. If they're stressed, you won't see them do that.
- Don't pat animals; stroke them.
- A two-hour ride will calm down an animal more than a one-hour ride. Bumpy roads are stressful.
- Calm animals are easier to handle. Screaming and yelling is really stressful to animals. Screaming and yelling versus gate slamming? Animals know the difference. They know the screaming and yelling is directed at them.
- Whites of the eyes, nostrils flaring, tail swishing—these are all signs that the animal is stressed.
- All grazing animals need to be in social group. How we raise them is how they become problematic.
- Sheep are super followers. "It's like siphoning water," Grandin said. "They flow."
- Calm animals gain more weight.
- Dairy cows decrease milk production if they're being yelled at and hit.
- A lone animal will run over you. Work them in groups of threes or so.
- New things are attractive when an animal is allowed to voluntarily approach it, and scary when they are suddenly or forcefully introduced.
- There is different baggage for animals who have been rescued. Starved horses don't have fear memories. But abused horses do.

COWBOYS AND LOBSTERMEN

I n his best-selling book, *The Secret Life of Lobsters*, Trevor Corson calls lobstermen "cowboys of the American East." I've been mulling over that phrase for years, contemplating the parallels of cowboys on the range and lobstermen on the water:

- Physical strength
- Acquired wisdom and patience
- Danger in the form of calculated as well as unforeseen risks
- Working with the elements

And that's just a start.

I was born and raised in Maine. I've been clamming and done plenty of fishing. But I've never been lobstering. That is, not until one recent summer when my friend, Rick Hollingshead, bowed to my nagging and let me join him. Rick lobsters the waters of Quahog Bay off Harpswell. He's been hauling since he was four when he first headed out with his father.

Just like cowboys, lobstermen can have a deep understanding and even compassion for the animals they harvest. They must tolerate the government's regulation of their livelihood. They work through their day with an immense and impressive repertoire of physical skills and honed muscle memory.

Hollingshead took horseman Elijah Moore and me out on the water. Elijah grew up in Utah. As many years as he has in the saddle, Rick has at sea. At about age ten, Rick set up traps of his own. He'd bike down to his skiff with bait bags full of mackerel and herring, dangling off the handlebars.

He's in his fifties now and works a twenty-foot lobster boat with a 90-horse outboard. For years, he had a thirty-five-footer. This new, used boat is quicker, requires less maintenance, and uses much less gas.

Elijah and I watch as Rick deftly maneuvers the boat to pick us up from a wharf near Cundy's Harbor. It lightly touches the dock, and he keeps it steady as we clamor aboard. One of us does something inappropriate, and he shakes his head, "Oh, I don't want a Joner coming out with me." A Joner. As in Davey Jones's locker. As in bad luck.

Some lobstermen are awful superstitious. Rick worked as a sternman for one of them.

- Never ever flip a hatch upside down. Once, when he did accidentally, they went out hauling anyway. All hell broke loose. They were lucky to get home alive.
- Never bring pork on board. Never squeal like a pig. Never even talk about pigs. (And I'd brought BLTs for lunch.)

Elijah laughed. Cowboys, it seems, can be suspicious too. He recalled his grandfather, a Texas Ranger and one of the first to work cattle in Utah. "Something happened when my granddad was in Texas," he told us, "and from then on, he would never turn around if he forgot something. It didn't matter what it was, there was no turning around. And that's been passed down through the family. There's no going back, ever."

Rick set about his business of hauling traps. If he was a rider, you'd be watching a ranch versatility performance at every buoy. He'd maneuver the boat so that each buoy appeared within easy reach on the starboard side. In the thirty seconds it took to grab and haul, Rick would have his hands on the throttle, the wheel, the shifter, the line to the trap, and the lever for the hydraulic hauler. With his eyes, he would watch the hauler, the line, the water and how the boat was shifting as the weight of the trap affected it.

One trap, sometimes two, if he'd set a double line, were brought effortlessly to the sideboard. Most often, there were lobsters inside. Most often, many were tossed overboard.

Keepers must have a body between 3¼ to 5 inches in length. Any lobster measuring more or less must be returned to the sea. Any female with eggs must be returned. Any female with a notched tail must be returned.

The lobster trap itself is not a particularly tricky mechanism, explained Rick. "They've put cameras on the traps…You should see the lobsters going in and out."

For eight years (the length of time it takes to mature to 3¼ inches), lobsters learn there is little consequence for entering: They get fed. They get hauled. They get tossed back into the ocean.

"We take good care of them," he said.

I thought of my boat companion, Elijah. A while back, I was watching him work with a horse. The horse was ten feet behind him, but Elijah could still see her with his peripheral vision. He wanted her to stay put while he talked with me.

The horse wanted to be close to him. (All horses want to be close to Elijah.) She started to take a step forward. Elijah set her back with the slightest move of his right shoulder. His shoulder! That's feel.

It took a small mistake made by Rick Hollingshead for me to recognize a parallel intuition. He had just sent a trap off the sideboard and into the sea. Then he glanced at his depth finder and hauled it back up, shaking his head. "You gotta have these traps set just right. If you're three feet off, you won't get lobster. What happened there was the bottom came up real quick on me. No good."

To me, it was like all the other traps he'd set that day. I didn't see anything wrong.

But while Rick was chatting, fixing bait, watching the current and moving the boat, he was also lining things up for the perfect trap setting: about forty feet down on a slope with plenty of rocks and kelp.

Once he had the trap back on the sideboard, he spun the boat around and placed it right where he wanted it. "That's good fishing there," he said, satisfied. "Lotta hiding for the lobsters."

Great horsemen and horsewomen notice horses' movements and signs before the rest of us. They get more from their horses because they see the softness and see them try before the rest of us do. They offer the release and the reward before the rest of us would too.

Similarly, Rick doesn't see Quahog Bay like I do. I look at the surface and ins and outs of all the pretty little coves and picturesque islands. I notice the wind when it blows in my face. My vision is two-dimensional stuff compared to what Rick takes in.

He talked about the lobsters' movement during the summer. "Lobsters shed at fifty-three degrees. They come up in the channels to shed. Then they lay low, hang out, and harden up before heading back out the bay. They'll survive on their own meat 'til their shells get hard and they can come out again."

Rick sees all this action in his head. He doesn't need a fancy underwater camera. He senses the wind picking up before the rest of us see white caps forming. After more than forty years on the water, his trap-to-keeper ratio is better than most. Yet he's still always learning. How? The lobsters and the sea show him. Just like the horses show Elijah. If he's not catching them, he adjusts.

As the season progresses, he will move his traps more offshore. He might switch up his bait, depending on the trap's location or time of year.

As for the day-to-day adjustments and risks he faces, Rick says, "Common sense goes a long way. Mother Nature, she'll beat you down." Spoken like a true cowboy.

Rick set the bait and let go of another trap. We've watched him haul some hundred traps so far.

"How the heck do you remember where they all are?" asks Elijah. Rick just smiled. "You just do."

Sidebar

When not lobstering, Rick serves as a caretaker for a large Cundy's Harbor property. He does everything there—maintaining the buildings and boats, harvesting timber, landscaping. But the last thing he thought he'd be doing was hugging horses.

Rick's boss brought horses to the property some five years ago. I was called to help this non-horseman learn the basics of safe handling and management.

Rick was edgy around horses. When they snorted, he jumped. When they spooked, he spooked more. When they got their hooves trimmed, he gagged at the smell. (He was, however, unfazed by the stench of bait.)

But talk about a quick study. It wasn't long before Rick was on his own, managing all the challenges with intelligence and sensitivity. Not only did he master horse care, he came to love it. With perhaps a coffee or beer in hand, Rick has come to spend many a quiet moment just hanging with the horses at the barn.

He called me the other day. He wanted me to know about the passing of Cupcake, a big, gentle Clydesdale-thoroughbred cross.

A vet came. The owner attended. Rick told them he couldn't be there for it. He paused before telling me, "I said to them, 'You wouldn't want to see a grown man cry, now would you?'"

Hang in there, Rick. We know your pain.

FOUR:

Places & Travels

DUBLIN, IRELAND

When the boys were young, we spent a year in Dublin, Ireland. It was 1996 and we lived on Dublin's gritty north side in a lower-middle class neighborhood.

There was a small sector of horse ownership and care that was very different than I'd ever seen. Carefree and haphazard, these so-called urban cowboys were glamorized in the movie, *The Commitments*, when one character brought his horse up the elevator of his subsidized housing unit. Others considered this horse population a big problem, especially from a sanitation and animal welfare issue.

Sometimes, horses just roamed. Sometimes, they were staked out in public parks. Their owner had tied them by halter and length of rope to a metal stake, pounded into the ground.

For the most part, everyone just left them alone. Sometimes, kids would hop on bareback, regardless of who it belonged to (if it belonged to anyone). It never fazed anyone that ownership of these horses was so ill-defined. For hours and days, the horses would roam or stay staked out without water. I was upset.

But then I looked at their condition. They were fine, well-mannered horses in good condition. None were ribby, lame, or with skin conditions. They seemed unfazed by their situation. So, why should I be getting my knickers in a twist?

NATIONAL COWBOY POETRY GATHERING
Elko, Nevada

During the week-long National Cowboy Poetry Gathering in Elko, Nevada, thousands of fans leaned in to catch every nuance of recitation as the world's best cowboy poets took turns on stage. The *Western Folklife* event is the granddaddy of gatherings, a week in which the genre's best poets, artists, and musicians fill the convention center, schools, bars, and museum galleries with their talents.

Soaking up their performances is an exercise in joyous fulfillment. It's like going to church where cowboy life is the celebrated religion. Not a believer? The sheer passion and energy here will convert you. It was backstage where I had the most mind-expanding moments.

Poet Vess Quinlan recalled when the gathering was just getting started in the mid-1980s. He remembered a young *Los Angeles Times* journalist complaining that his boss had sent him to a reporter's Siberia. What was there to cover at this obscure event in northern Nevada? Who cares about a bunch of ranch guys reciting old campfire yarns?

They watched together as an old timer took the stage and started into a classic. Softly and passionately, he carried the audience through the story. Then suddenly, he stopped. He'd gotten lost in the verse.

In front, there sat a row of young buckaroos. One of them picked up the line and helped the elder man return to the words. It was a quiet, compassionate gesture, like opening the door for a friend. More significantly, it was oral history defined.

In that moment, the reporter realized why he was there. He'd found his story.

For natives to the ranch lifestyle, the gathering is like a family reunion, a reaffirmation of all that matters in life. For those less steeped in the culture, it offers impressions and translations far more compelling and accurate than country songs, Marlboro ads, and tough truck commercials.

"The event is a myth buster. These are real people. Real culture," said Randy Rieman, one of the event's most popular artists. For sure, many would agree when Rieman added, "I've never been able to think about poetry without the word 'cowboy' in front of it."

Fellow poet Wallace McRae laughed at the stereotype when asked about it. "If you're a cowboy, you should be completely inarticulate. Shuffle your feet around for a while. Say, 'Yes, ma'am. No, ma'am.'"

In truth, they can be sentimental, intellectual, thoughtful, and eloquent. It's no wonder that the National Endowment for the Arts has bestowed cowboy poets with awards and fellowships.

Poet and accomplished horseman Joel Nelson wrote this poem, as brief as it is beautiful in relating how poetry itself takes shape.

While I Sleep

While I sleep
Words come in the night
Like small birds and critters
Along dusty trails
Through the branches
Over rocky stream beds
To line up and watch me
Waiting for me to awaken
Looking at one another
Shifting
Trading places
Rearranging themselves
As though they somehow know
Their proper order

And what they need to say
Sometimes I awaken
And acknowledge them on paper
As I should
If not
They dissolve back into the shadows
The thickets
The burrows
And if they ever appear again
Will they all be the same ones
And will the order be disturbed

ANXIOUS WHEN AWAY

Am I the only one who gets stressed when away from the herd? Are you as comfortable in a crowd or a city as you are kicking around the barn?

This past week had me first at the Equine Affaire in Springfield, Massachusetts, and then on to New Jersey to see my son in a NCAA championship soccer match.

The Equine Affaire was darn fun. And the game was thrilling. But all along there was an undercurrent of unease:

- How are my horses doing?
- Did my friend remember to close that gate?
- It's deer season and Sunday. I should be out in the woods riding!
- My boots smell like asphalt, not manure. Something's wrong.

This country girl malaise peaked with my George Washington Bridge episode in New York City. After my son's game, I got back on the New Jersey Turnpike and headed north. You would have noticed me. I was the one doing 60 mph, glancing desperately at road signs and trying valiantly to decipher my own hand-scrawled directions. Cars whizzed by on both sides. Someone honked.

Usually I'm in a car with Maine plates. Drivers are more sympathetic. "We can forgive her ineptitude. It's probably the first time she's seen stoplights. They have only dirt roads and stop signs up there." But I was using my friend's car with Connecticut plates.

Someone else honked at me. I knew I needed to get to the George Washington Bridge and felt relieved to get in the correct lane for it. But then: upper deck or lower deck? Does it matter? What happens if I choose the wrong one? I flipped a virtual coin, chose the lower deck, and bumbled on.

Then I started seeing the toll signs. Of course, I don't do anything sensible like EZ pass. With the booths looming four hundred yards ahead, I saw the cost: CARS - $12

What? I had money out and ready alright. I was figuring it'd be a few bucks. I had a few bucks. No more. Could I use a debit card? Could I back up to the last exit? Could I play the dumb farm girl from Maine? Could my cute dog riding shotgun help sweet-talk the attendant? Belle looked at me with those puppy-dog eyes, whimpered, and licked my face as if to say, "Yes. Yes, I can!"

I pulled up to the attendant and tried to hand her my two bucks and then offered my debit card. Belle put her little legs on my legs and leaned forward to plead the case. The woman shook her head and sternly put out her hand like a crossing guard directing a school kid not to cross. "Right now a camera is taking a picture of your license plate. They will contact your state's Department of Motor Vehicles and send you a bill."

Well, they weren't going to send a cop after me, drag me off in cuffs, and confiscate my dog and my friend's car.

And, heck, I didn't run out of gas. (Like the last time I was on Manhattan Island.)

I returned home and things were fine. The horses looked at me like I'd just gone in town on an errand. No big deal.

Do I want to go back to the Big City tomorrow? No, thanks. I like stinky clothes and muddy paddocks just fine.

WAR HORSE

For horse people, no theatrical, big city production beats *War Horse*. Lucky me to see it at Lincoln Center in New York City! Since I'd never been to a show in New York, any production would have dazzled and impressed. But with *War Horse*, the thrill was surreal.

On a stage under intense lights, watched by eleven hundred well-dressed theatergoers, in a building surrounded by skyscrapers and another eight million people, a team of three puppeteers brought me right back to my barn.

As the play opens, we see Joey, the horse and main character. He is played by three puppeteers—one in control of head movement, one in control of front legs, one in charge of his haunches and tail.

We watch Joey breathe, look around, swish his tail, flick his ears back and forth, and snort when something spooks him off stage.

Five minutes. No words. A horse being a horse. Five minutes and I was tearing up already.

The next two-and-a-half hours had me transfixed. But why? What I knew intuitively I couldn't answer formally until I dove into the program notes and read about the author of *War Horse* and the puppeteers who brought the horse to life on stage.

Initially a children's story, *War Horse* was written by Michael Morpurgo. Back in the 1970s, Morpurgo searched for a way to honor family members who had suffered and died during World War I, a war which claimed the lives of twenty million people and eight million horses.

At the same time, Morpurgo and his wife were running Farms for City Children, an educational charity where city kids can visit and work on English farms.

One night, he met a seven-year-old boy who stammered and was so taunted by his peers that he'd given up on speaking. Morpurgo watched the boy as he hung out in the barn after dinner. The boy was talking freely to a horse. He was confident, knowing he wasn't going to be judged or mocked, explained the author.

So, Morpurgo knew a thing or two about the therapeutic powers of animals and the intense, non-verbal bond we develop with them.

Those points form the spine of *War Horse*. A horse saves a boy and the boy saves the horse.

Now enter the puppeteers. I'm not talking about Kermit. Puppets like Kermit "aren't really animals. They simply use the shape of an animal to add some kind of texture to what is basically a human argument," said Adrian Kohler, co-creator of the *War Horse* puppets. "Working with the horses in *War Horse* has meant we've got to learn how horses think, how horses are different from humans."

War Horse puppeteers were so skilled you forgot they were there. You never saw them breathe. You saw the horse breathe. You never saw them fidget. You saw Joey shift his weight, shake his tail, scratch an itch with his teeth, stomp his hooves. Joey's movements were believable because the puppeteers' lack of movement was so committed. As Kohler said, "It's sort of the Zen of non-movement.

You move only when you know that you're adding to the meaning of the moment."

Joey is no Mr. Ed. I suspended my disbelief wholeheartedly.

MIDWEST MOVE

What started as an idea materialized gradually and came to fruition as I moved myself and my barnyard (four horses, two dogs, one cat) to Iowa. Yes, Iowa. It was exciting, stressful, and successful.

Before last week, my longest haul was a one-day, twelve-hour gig to Connecticut and back with two horses. This trip was twice the journey with twice the horses, and it required lots of advanced organization, fingernail-biting, coffee, and toll money.

It was quite a process as I first contemplated the dreaded empty nest (left by my three growing sons) and then worked with friends and family to make things happen. Just now, I'm sitting on my new back porch, contemplating the long physical and mental journey. The horses are grazing lazily. Dogs are at my feet. And the indoor cat is busy monitoring the sparrow nest just outside the window.

Though I love my native state dearly, I also love exploring, discovering, and challenging myself.

It was a big decision. Big decisions can be broken down into bits. There are emotional bits, practical bits, family bits, financial bits. Moving horses across country itself was a decision full of bits, especially the practical ones. And they needed to be ironed out well in advance. The horses would need to be healthy and prepared. The rig would have to be safe and solid. The route would have to be researched. The destination point would have to be ready for us.

Dr. Rachel Flaherty visited the girls within a month of departure. They'd need spring shots, health certificates, and Coggins tests. To complete most interstate travel, horses need a Coggins within the year and a health certificate within the month. Some states, most particularly Florida, may require more. I talked with Flaherty and Iowa officials and checked with my friend in Ohio, too, where we'd stay overnight. It's expensive stuff. Vet work for all four came to about eight hundred bucks.

After much deliberation, we decided to upgrade our truck and trailer rig from a bumperpull to a gooseneck. We thought the investment would make the hauling safer and more comfortable. In hindsight, I'd say it was wholly worthwhile.

We packed for emergencies of all kinds:

- ✓ Truck: a trailer spare, a truck spare, jacks and irons for flats of both kinds, jumper cables. We had contact numbers for our memberships in USRider and AAA.
- ✓ Water, hay, and hay stretcher (as loose horse treats), banamine, bute, Gas-Ex, extra halters and leads, electrolyte replacement pastes, and much more.
- ✓ First aid kit for us, cell phones, maps, and lots of healthy snacks, drinks, overnight bags.

How much can you prepare a horse for a life-altering move? They would be trailering farther than any of them had ever trailered. Plus, they'd be moving from minimal grass to round-the-clock grass.

No, I didn't sit them all down for a long talk, with a PowerPoint presentation, coffee, and Kleenex. But I did load and haul all four several times, putting two fore and aft the center wall. It got to be a comfortable, stress-free process with each horse stepping on and off without hesitation. They were hauled free and so were able to move around and get their heads down for hay.

It being spring in Maine, there wasn't too much I could do about grazing. But for weeks, I hand-grazed them for a few hours a day while my lawnmower remained in hibernation.

In Iowa, Steve readied the horse quarters with a new run-in shed and fortified fencing, keeping in mind the escape antics of one herd member in particular. We also lined up a local vet in case we had any issues after arriving.

My friend Michelle Melaragno, my dad, and Steve all helped with the planning for the twelve-hundred-mile drive. I'd contemplated driving straight through with no overnight stop. They all thought otherwise. Am I glad we stopped! The trip's toll on my brain and body was much greater than I reckoned.

Before 5:00 a.m. on May 17, we loaded up and pulled out of the driveway, mostly awake and full of nervous energy but secure with the knowledge that we'd prepared as well as we could have.

We were off and away before the sun touched my dear Brunswick barn. A caravan of sorts: Dad pulled a U-haul tagalong behind his pickup. My dogs rode shotgun with him.

The four horses had loaded easily and shuffled for position in the gooseneck. I sat behind the wheel while my friend, Michelle, organized maps, snacks, and sipped on coffee. The cat, wedged between foodstuffs, backpacks, and suitcases, meowed and settled down in her crate.

Riding in tandem, we made an early and wise decision: Let's NOT stay in visual contact. We all had different needs regarding eats, bathroom breaks, and animals. Stopping for all of them in unison would waste time. Dad tended to drive a bit more slowly, and we coffee-guzzling gals needed to stop more often. Cell phones allowed us to remain in close contact. Indeed, the separation of a few miles proved helpful as we warned each other of scares, accidents, and jams.

MAINE TO IOWA, CONTINUED

By rough estimate, I've driven across country and back more than a dozen times. At age twenty, I drove non-stop, alone, in my little Subaru, drinking Big Gulps full of Tab and Mello Yello and stopping in rest areas and truck stops for catnaps.

For nearly ten summers, I traveled with my young sons to and from Montana. Once, we were six in a Toyota station wagon in the summer heat without air conditioning and lived to tell about it.

My confidence was backed by these hearty experiences. Heck, if I can do five-hundred-mile days full of whining, backseat toddler wrestling matches, and crowded, cheap motel rooms, what's two days to Iowa?

Turns out I'm older and more tired. Turns out hauling four thousand pounds of precious cargo adds a whole new element of fatigue and stress to a road trip.

Transporting horses means you look at every angle of the drive with a more serious level of risk management. Will this brisk wind on the open road jostle us? Will this traffic jam combined with the hot weather mean the horses overheat?

Every acceleration or braking is made knowing four animals would be bracing for and leaning into the changes. Every car or truck, until proven otherwise, is considered a potential threat or hazard. To pass or be passed used to be a simple, routine gesture. Now, it was loaded with exit strategy and safety concerns.

Don't get me wrong. We had fun. But it was a serious drive; I held the steering wheel at ten and two o'clock and felt like a sixteen-year-old with a learner's permit.

Somewhere in Ohio, we shook our heads as a rusty pickup truck pulled onto the highway. The guys were hauling a rickety flatbed trailer with wood and metal side panels. The four-foot panels were flapping back and forth. Michelle, who has years of hauling experience and a commercial driver's license, was at the wheel. We laughed that we should take a picture and send it to Drs. Tomas and Rebecca Gimenez who run TLAER and keep a photo library of unsafe trailer rigs.

Suddenly, one of those panels whipped out of its anchors and sailed in our general direction. You can't swerve when hauling a load like ours. I held my breath as Michelle narrowly avoided what could have been a disastrous flying object encounter.

The driver looked back, shrugged his shoulders and chuckled with his buddy. We decided to pass these clowns as quickly as possible but not before calling my dad and letting him know about his upcoming road hazard.

It was after 9:00 p.m., after getting the dogs walked and horses settled in their overnight quarters (a friend's small arena with plenty of hay and water), when we stumbled into the Maple City Tap in Chardon, Ohio, for dinner. Food. Any kind of food would do. A drink would be good, too. We ordered and relished the success of six hundred miles behind us. We listened as a few bar patrons sang along to the jukebox's Johnny Cash song. Really. It was as comfortably casual as the day was not.

NEW HOME FOR THE HERD

Around dinnertime after a second twelve-hour driving day (nearly all on Interstate 80), we pulled into the horses' new home. It's a century-old homestead with a modest farmhouse and nine acres of fenced pasture.

In the month before our arrival, Steve oversaw the construction of a 50x100-foot paddock, removal of a long stretch of four-strand, barbed-wire fencing, and the placement of a run-in shed to add to the shelter of the small barn. The set-up is darned-near perfect, in my mind. It is safe, minimal, efficient, and includes my favorite feature— a slip space, allowing us to move through and letting no gate ever be forgotten.

We off-loaded the horses and let them loose in the paddock. All ears, eyes, and noses got busy taking in their new environment.

I filled buckets, thinking the automatic waterer might stump them. Hardly. They ignored my water buckets and stood in line to use it.

We let them graze on the small amount of paddock grass until the next morning when they got their first honest turnout since last fall. We limited their pasture time to a few hours and kept our eyes out for loose poops and achy bellies for those first few days. Maybe those weeks of hand-grazing paid off. Maybe they're just easy keepers. Either way, the shift to grass was seamless.

While the horses sussed things out, I cleaned and cleared the new digs. The previous owner was a carpenter with ducks, chickens, alpacas, and horses. The stall area had a foot of old, dried multi-species manure. I carted a dozen loads to my newly-established manure pile, then I replaced it with limestone gravel.

There was plenty of room for tack, but first I had to empty the space of pallets, bundles of shingles, more manure, straw, and wood scraps. Dangerous nails and screws (for hanging his tools) were everywhere. Cobwebs got swept down. I found a garbage bin half full of old dog food and a half dozen mice who'd gotten in, gorged on the chow, then perished when they couldn't get back out. Lovely.

After two days, I was beginning to have a handle on how the space could serve us. I hung bridles, rope halters, and my tool belt. I brought in the saddles, grooming supplies, first aid kit, and other gear.

Two simple and vital feel-good elements of my old barn came with me: an old wooden box (safe to have around horses and great to sit on) and my dumpster-salvaged radio. They've traveled with me from barn to barn and bring me comfort in more ways than one.

The place was beginning to shape up. It was time for the first ride.

DEBUT OUTING

I got out for my first Iowa ride on a warm, windy, sunny day. After some discussion, Pep and I managed to head down the gravel road away from her shrieking herd mates. She was antsy and her trot felt a bit like a lopsided jackhammer.

We live near the Hawkeye Wildlife Management Area, a fourteen-thousand-acre mix of woods, field, and marshland. Farmers lease land and plant corn, wheat, and soybeans in scattered fields. Deer and pheasant hunters love it. At first glance, I did too.

There are small parking lots every half mile or so, and I cut into every one we encountered. Trails lead to fields, stands of hardwood, or both. After following one trail, I came upon a small quiet pond. Quiet, that is, until it exploded with ducks, beautiful wood ducks, at least ten pairs. One after another, they took off and circled over the trees.

Another trail led to a small field of solid white clover. Felt like I was in *Alice in Wonderland*. Or a clandestine Provincetown. We stumbled upon a gathering place for local gay men. Not sure how they've interpreted 'wildlife management,' but the naked men were perfectly friendly anyway.

A quarter million people live within twenty-five miles, but you'd never know it. The closest town, Swisher, has a population of seven hundred eighty-one. Make that seven hundred eighty-two. Yahoo.

No ride with Maddy and Pep would be complete without a good dose of bushwhacking. And unintentionally, we got more than our share. We were climbing along the side of another lovely pond, and the brush was getting thicker and thicker. I got off, and we ducked and bobbed toward more open ground. Finally, we got to the edge of another field, but it was bordered by four strands of old, tangled barbed wire.

About face! The return to the pond got a little hairy. We had a close, intimate introduction to those thorny, strong-as-hell vines that clasp trees and hang vertically, diagonally, and wherever you'd rather they not.

Let's just say I was REALLY glad I had a great horse that stood patiently as I hacked away at a vine that bound her hind leg and then her front leg. Pep was a trooper. (My Gerber knife wasn't the perfect implement, but we would have been screwed without it.)

It was quite a first ride. We got home dirty, sweaty, thirsty, and eager to explore more.

A SECOND LOOK

With experience comes confidence. So, with one big ride behind us, the pony and I were game for anything. Bring it! Iowa brought a banquet.

The second ride started with a shriek. We were all set: tacked up, bottle of water tied to the saddle, treats in my jean jacket. I reached for my armitas. A black spider, as big as my fist, crawled out from them and scurried toward my leg.

Now, I'm not a killer, but I made an exception here. Then I took another five minutes to look for any of his family members. Maine doesn't have big, black, hairy spiders.

We got going and headed down the county road—a long, mostly straight road that leads through miles of Hawkeye Wilderness Management area along the Iowa River.

It can be a busy road with farmers and boaters driving fast and trailering all kinds of equipment. They were unfazed by horse and rider. But the new sounds of truck and trailer on gravel rattled Pep. So did the random rocks flying out from their tires. And the thick plume of dust enveloping us as they passed was also an unfamiliar phenomenon.

And then there was the firing range. I have a whole new respect for Mounted Cowboy Shooters and their fine horses. Dozens of gun owners visit this firing range every day to get in their target practice. They shoot with everything from revolvers to assault rifles. It sits right next to the road. There is no going around it.

We managed to move past but not without ample discussion. There was a bit more deliberation when we discovered the shotgun and archery range at the next mile.

Behind the archery range, we found a huge swath of field bordered by woods and water. Some fields were full of wheat, and many had soybeans and corn on the way. Those farmers used mighty big equipment—two stories high, with big shiny teeth and mammoth tires.

Water crossings were the least of our concerns.

But along with the rich soil of the flood plain comes fabulous footing for riding. We trotted past cottonwoods and listened to scores of birds: Orioles, cardinals, indigo buntings, towhees, meadowlarks, vesper sparrows, cowbirds, and blackbirds all make their homes here.

We stopped for snacks and lingered in the sandy footing of an Iowa River tributary.

At one point, we followed a path through a belly-high field of wheat right near the Iowa River. We met a man bow-fishing for carp. It was sport, he said. "No one really easts carp," he told me, then pointed up river to a tree where a large bird perched. "Except for the eagle; he'll probably be down here in ten minutes, grabbing what I caught."

Pep can live up to her name. When the road is open and friendly, she finds stopping or even going slow distasteful. On this ride, once we started galloping, she saw no need for any other gait. Slowing her with no rein contact is a work in progress, so I was thankful for the space to slow by pulling her around in a circle.

On our Maine rides, we had more natural barriers. Maine has trees. Lots of them. They smell great and provide a woodsy intimacy to our rides. We get good at hugging horses' necks as we duck low branches. We push off from tree trunks as we pass so our kneecaps won't get crushed.

But apparently, we're not in Maine anymore.

HORSE-FRIENDLY OPEN SPACE

Horses need space. Riders do too. If you look at Swisher, Iowa, by satellite, you'll see lots of open space. When I moved here from Maine, I was excited to explore the nearby Hawkeye Wildlife Management Area. I did. It was wonderful until I got a ticket. I was cited for riding my horse on public land and fined $100.

Turns out the Hawkeye Wildlife Management Area is reserved for hunters and fishers. Despite the negligible environmental impact (Hoof prints? Occasional poop?) and acts of good citizenship (calling in poachers, carcass dumpers, litterers, etc.), I was labeled persona non grata by the Department of Natural Resources.

The citation left this horsewoman frustrated and curious about the state of horse-friendly public space. Iowa ranks forty-ninth out of fifty when it comes to the percentage of publicly owned land. One percent of its land consists of parks, forests, and grasslands. Horse riders are unwelcome on most of them. Maine, as some of you will attest, isn't much better. It ranks thirty-seventh.

Many of us enjoy riding on private land owned by friendly neighbors. But as time marches on, development often turns old trails into subdivisions, fields into fenced and gated backyards. Increasingly, we must resort to trailering to open space or riding around and around and around in an arena. It's a drag. For those of us with an open-space craving, it can be downright depressing.

But consider Utah. The state boasts five national parks and has a greater percentage of public land than every other state except Nevada and Alaska. Combine that with a culture that welcomes, embraces, and accommodates horse riders.

If a chance ever came to move there, what trail rider wouldn't jump at the opportunity?

That chance has arrived and this girl is Utah-bound.

THE HAUL TO UTAH

The lofty plan to move to Utah assumed the very real form of three trucks pulling out of Swisher, Iowa, and heading west.

Day One
With my dogs riding shotgun, I took the lead, pulling four horses in our gooseneck stock trailer. Brothers Bill and Steve Kueter followed

with the pony and mule in their bumperpull. Steve held up the rear in his SUV.

It was barely dawn as we pulled onto Interstate 80. The highway here is straight, flat, and fast. For one stretch of seventy-two miles, it doesn't deviate left or right by more than a yard.

While at the wheel, I spent the day reminiscing about good times in the Hawkeye state. We met some fine folks and explored some beautiful country.

Our humble convoy crossed Nebraska uneventfully, and around sunset we pulled into Big Springs (population four hundred and six), near the Colorado border.

The horses seemed happy for solid ground. They rolled, drank, and dug into flakes of hay. We headed up the highway to the only motel around, across the state line in Julesburg, Colorado.

In another week, said the front desk lady at the Platte Valley Inn, we wouldn't have gotten a room. That's when bird season starts, and the place fills with upland game hunters.

Her comment helped explain the curious sign in each room, admonishing guests: DO NOT CLEAN BIRDS IN ROOM!

Day Two

The next day started beautifully calm. The horses loaded without fuss, and again we drove with the sun rising directly behind us.

My mom is a photographer who lived in Montana for ten years. She always said the light plays differently here than back East. It's not easy to describe but easy to see, especially on a clear morning like this one.

Tension soon replaced calm for me as we reached Interstate 80's highest point of eighty six hundred feet and started the descent into Laramie, Wyoming. New England hauling offered no good preparation for the Rockies. With the weight of four horses in tow, I felt like a feeble security officer, trying to keep a football team from rushing the field. Fog, freezing temperatures, blowing snow, and heavy semi traffic only heightened my anxiety, but we managed.

The country, which James Galvin celebrated in his book, *The Meadow*, was just as he described it—stark, beautiful, and nearly uninhabited.

By the afternoon of our second day, we had a thousand miles behind us. The big climb and curvy descent into Salt Lake City lay ahead, and I was more than willing to let my friend, Bill, take over the driving.

I've spent summers and winters out West but never autumn. The landscape, dotted with yellow scrub oaks, cedars, junipers, and aspens, is as spectacular as any New England panorama. Here, though, the exposed geologic formations add another brilliant dimension. They reveal layers of reds, browns, yellows, and greys. Splendid dirt and stone rainbows.

We wove through the Salt Lake City and Provo traffic to land in Payson, a town of twenty thousand in Utah Valley. At West Field's Ranch, we settled the horses into their temporary digs.

That Utah idea? Like a phrase written in beach sand, it just got washed away by a big wave of reality. We're here. We're here!

LOOKING BACK, LOOKING FORWARD

I was born and raised on the coast of Maine. The ocean was a given. We swam in it, sailed on it, clammed it, fished it, even hopped its icebergs during the coldest winters.

Then I left home. When I came back years later, I was stunned by the beauty I'd taken for granted: The thick evergreen woods practically pushing themselves off seaside cliffs; the craggy shorelines, full of coves and inlets; those coves and inlets revealing eddies and tide pools; eddies and tide pools rich with life. I saw those things back then. I'm sure. But the beauty and details were newly captivating.

Now, I live in Utah and wake up every day, staring at the mountains: The ridges and draws marked with scrub oaks, junipers, and cacti; the canyons' spectacular dirt and rock color spectrum; the quiet spiked with calls of ravens and coyotes; the morass of life squeezed from this high, dry climate.

I feel fortunate to take in the state with non-native eyes and ears.

FIRST UTAH TRAIL RIDES

With a beautiful day beckoning and the sun on its downward trek, Pep and I followed a notion and headed out. I've had my eye on a nearby hill, wanting to reach the top.

Last week, Comet and I had made it up part way with Steve and Jodi. But as we're learning, hills here are like slices of cheesecake—it's often challenging to take it all in without feeling the effects, especially with a foot of snow.

On this return trip, we trotted through scrub oak and juniper and made it to that previous turnaround point in no time. Then, the pony and I continued up the largely treeless grade, spotting crisscrossing coyote and deer tracks.

What I hadn't realized from a distance was part of that cheesecake effect: the hill got awfully steep, awfully quick. With less than a quarter mile to the peak, I got off and walked with Pep through the crusty snow.

We reached the peak after thirty minutes of huffing, puffing, starts and stops. It was exhilarating. For the whole climb, we had been laboring in the shade, ascending the vertical east side. On the sixty-eight-hundred-foot summit, we stepped into the bright sun as if stepping onto a stage.

We caught our breaths, had a celebratory snack, and walked around in circles to take in three counties' worth of view. The remaining minutes of sun bathed us in its warmth and glow. The hill's peacefulness embraced us.

Neither of us is keen on steep downhills. We took a more gradual route home, following another ridge and then bushwacking through junipers. Dusk found us home, happy, and tired.

TERRAIN MAKES US NIMBLER

In human terms, they'd be golfers-turned-soccer players. That's the adjustment and improved athleticism of the herd with the move to Utah.

The terrain here is rocky and vertical. Our so-called pasture is anything but pastoral. Sage and juniper dominate. Grass competes with cacti for ground space. (We feed hay year-round.)

Add ice and snow and the horses sometimes have a heckuva time getting around. Lately, moving around the six acres has been a game of Chutes & Ladders; the horses pick and choose their routes or suffer the consequences. However, there is this huge silver lining: All the horses have become fitter, more agile, and savvier in the process.

Shea, in particular, seems to have benefited from the change. In Maine and Iowa, she was prone to hoof abscesses and lameness. The habitat here has toughened up her feet and forced a sort of physical therapy on her. I believe she's built strength and muscled herself way away from her prior issues.

Effects of terrain on the horse & rider partnership

Carrying riders in this terrain has taught our horses to be more nimble, too. They hunker down hills better and pay more attention to where they're stepping.

Along sheer ridges, especially, it can be tempting to take up the reins and try to tell them where to go. *Big mistake.* They always fare better with no head restriction and with the rider saying to them, "I trust you to steer a true course."

As a rider, I feel I'm on a fitter and more balanced horse. And working, riding, and hiking here have made us humans fitter and more balanced too. As for equipment, I'm thankful for leggings and a sturdy hat. Even established trails regularly require us to move through rough brush. My jeans would get shredded, if not for armitas.

As for low limbs and dense timber, the horses again are in charge of navigation. Just hug their necks and keep your head down 'til the coast is clear!

FIVE:

Work with Horses

CATCH-ABILITY

When I see haltered horses in a field, I cringe and then make two presumptions: 1) Their owner can't "catch" them, and 2) it's only a matter of time before those horses hurt themselves.

Catch-ability

Good owners invest time working with their horses so they like being around humans. It doesn't need to be warm and fuzzy. But at the very least, one should be able to approach the horse without much fuss.

There are as many training techniques for approach and catch-ability as there are clinicians, but most ideas come down to what Elijah Moore taught me years ago: Horses seek comfort. If you can offer it to them on a reliable basis, they'll come to you or at least let you come to them.

Don't want to invest the hours? Then perhaps refine your roping technique or have really yummy treats.

I used to think 'field safe' or leather halters were OK. That was before I did a little research and came to the conclusion that any halter can get horses in trouble.

Here's a test:

- Take the plastic ring from a milk jug cap or a cheap bracelet.
- Walk your field and scrutinize your barn space with these rings, running them across surfaces and sticking them everywhere from ground level to over your head.
- Do they stick or get caught anywhere?

Chances are your fencing alone represents a big enough hazard for haltered horses.

Another hazardous practice: Cross-tying

Steady, well-trained horses give to pressure. But it's stressful for a horse to give to pressure only to run into more pressure. That happens with crossties. A horse might find it can escape pressure by going up, but that can yield tragic results. It's not hard to see why even calm horses can panic in crossties. Crosstie mechanics don't allow the horse to investigate things by adjusting its head and putting both eyes on the pressure sources.

Last week I talked with a big-time director in the horse world. She told me how sad she was at having to put down her faithful, steady trail horse after he injured himself on crossties. Argh!

Here's what Julie Goodnight says about crossties: "Crossties can be one of the most dangerous ways to tie a horse…According to the dictionary as written by the horse, crossties are a gymnastic apparatus.

"Never medicate, treat, fly spray or do anything else that might cause a horse discomfort or alarm when he is tied hard and fast. Especially not in crossties, which are, after all, an apparatus for doing back flips. That would be dangerous and could initiate a catastrophic chain of events."

Warwick Schiller cautions that, like horse trailers and spade bits, they're no good for unprepared horses. I'd like to think tie bars would be a safer alternative. Schiller uses crossties but prepares and teaches the horse about them first. "The crosstie itself is not the problem but a lack of preparation is," said Schiller in an email. "Just like with most issues people have with their horses, their lack of preparation causes the issue, not the 'thing' itself—trailer, lead change, crossties, tie pole, collection, standing still, etc., etc."

PADDOCK DESIGNS

When you finally sit down at night, are you completely sure you closed that gate or stall door? Did you take off that halter? Did you hang it up in the right spot, so you can grab it again tomorrow morning when it's still dark? Did you latch the latch? Did you leave the lights on or water running?

The list goes on. With horse care, it seems we're always performing several tiny chores and safety checks each time we visit our girls and boys. And we tend to do it all while simultaneously performing three other tasks.

Lately, I've been focusing on minimizing my room for error, especially when it comes to loose horses. Resident Escape Geniuses have compelled me to make some crucial paddock designs:

- The slip-through—a passage through which humans but no horse can pass. It measures the exact width of a five-gallon stall bucket but no wider.
- The divot: a dip in the ground on which rests the wheel of the main gate. Should the gate be left unchained, it will still be very difficult to simply push open. With the divot, one has to lift and push simultaneously. So far, the Houdinis have not figured out these mechanics.

As for lights and halter hooks? I know my hooks and handles well enough to use them in the dark. If I never turn on the light, I don't have to worry about leaving it on.

NOTES ON BROOKE

B rooke reminds me again how past traumas can impact animals forever, even when they're far removed from their bad situations. I don't know all the details. But I'm told she was kept in a 10x10-foot stall with three other horses for years. She gave birth to a foal in that stall, making it five.

I visited Brooke several times before adopting her, taking her to one of the agency's round pens, getting to know her, putting her through some elementary groundwork. I recognized her amazing try. Her eyes were not readily soft, but she gave me plenty of glimmers of potential.

Brooke learned at the rescue farm that not all humans are neglectful and abusive. She wanted to be with me and wanted to work with me. Taking her history into account, that attitude alone was a miracle. That she was sound was a bonus.

After some contemplation, Brooke came home to our farm. And then I quickly experienced the other side of this sweet girl. I received Brooke's baggage.

When it came to her stall and food delivery, the message was clear: Gimme or get outta my way! As soon as Brooke saw food coming her way, ears went back and hooves started dancing.

At first, I had trouble staying safe during those first feedings. So, instead of bringing the hay to her, I would place it in a closed stall hours beforehand. This strategy avoided the bad behavior. It was a non-confrontational stance and wasn't solving the problem. But it bought me some time to think.

I talked about her food-induced craziness with a few people, most notably trainer Chris Lombard. And I tried to put myself in her place. Before she was rescued, she was literally fighting for survival. Back then, Brooke learned that if she was aggressive, she might eat.

I'm the lead horse in her life now. I have to show her that she can have hay when I allow it. She needs to learn that she won't go hungry if she waits. She needs to learn that I won't hurt her. I stay consistent with every encounter and stick with the adage so familiar among trainers: Make it easy to do the right thing and hard to do the wrong thing.

There is a lot of 'unlearning' in this process too. It is NOT okay to be aggressive. It's NOT okay to dive at the hay as I am setting it down. It is NOT okay to invade my space.

I had great plans to spend these past months getting her used to being ridden. Instead, we devote our hours to real simple stuff. Each time I put a halter on her and have her do groundwork, I place hay within her reach. She can have it when I say so.

She's made wonderful progress. Each time I take the halter off and give her a rub to end the session, she never runs away. She always lingers, as if to say: 'Can I do something else for you?' Yup, that's one heckuva try, especially considering her baggage.

NOTES ON JODI

Jodi is a four-year-old quarter horse type, acquired from a kind Wisconsin owner. Conformation-wise, she's a tank. She has decent manners and came to us pretty much halter broke. We're challenged by bringing her knowledge and training in line with her impressive size and strength.

When Jodi first came to us, she landed firmly at the bottom of the herd. Peppermint, in particular, let the new girl know exactly where she belonged.

But Jodi has worked her way to the top. Or at least close to it. When hay is tossed, Jodi gets second dibs, after Brooke. I'm no expert at herd dynamics, but I have to think that it's a combination of naivety, confidence, and brute force that got her to where she is now.

She seems to say, 'Hey, happy to be here! But tell me to move and I'll kick your butt!' She used to say that with horses and humans alike. Now she just says it to her herd mates.

When we picked her up, we had a bit of a trailer-loading issue. As in, she wanted nothing to do with it. More than an hour later, we had her loaded alright. But it was a multi-person struggle and not a lot of fun for anyone, including Jodi.

So, one of the first things on my New Horse To Do list was trailer loading. I was determined to have it be happy trailer loading.

First, I put hay down for Peppermint in the front half of the trailer, loaded her, and closed the center wall. Then I put hay and grain down at the very front of the back section, seven feet from the step.

I brought Jodi from the paddock and let her check out the options. There was hay, grain, and a friend OR she could hang out on a hot gravel driveway. She was interested. She placed one hoof on the trailer floor and thought about it. At one point, with little bit of pressure, she teetered at the step. She brought her hind feet close and appeared ready to tip, fall, step, or leap into the trailer.

It was hot, and continuing would have been a struggle for all of us. So we stopped before it became a battle or a stressed situation. During the session, I realized she needed more work on responding to pressure-and-release cues and worked on them without involving the trailer.

Today, I reset the scene: Pep in the front section with hay; hay and grain in the trailer, just out of reach.

I asked Jodi to step up. She did. I asked her to come off. She seemed to say, 'I'm just fine here. Thanks.'

Feeling pretty good about this progress! Now we just have to make it routine, so when we really need to load up, it won't be an issue.

∾ — ∾

We're coming up to one month with Jodi. What a month! Over these few weeks, Jodi has used her size and attitude to significantly reshape the herd dynamics. She stayed at the bottom for about one minute and in the process has helped me to learn that herd rank works more like an algorithm than a simple linear, ladder-like formula.

She's also reminded me that young'uns are young'uns are young'uns. How many times do parents say, "Don't touch, Look with your eyes, not with your hands, Keep your hands to yourself"?

Jodi is the toddler in the gift shop. Setting the saddle on the fence? She will suss it out with her lips. Then she'll probably grab it with her teeth and pull it off the fence. Setting those granola bars out for the trail ride? She'll pick them up with her teeth. When she can't open them, she'll try stomping them open with her front hooves.

Needless to say, there are lessons to learn. For both of us.

∾ — ∾

It's fun working with a new horse. But it's a constant challenge. Each time we hit a roadblock, I ask myself if I'm doing right by her. My mind casts back to those thoughtful, patient, and effective horsemen and women I've had the privilege of watching. I try to channel them.

Trailer loading become a snap for Jodi.

On.

Turn around in the trailer.

Off.

Cake.

But what if I ask her to back off?

We tried it last weekend. I asked her gently and then a little more strongly. No luck. The most I got from her was one foot on the driveway, but then she'd chicken out and step forward.

I had to laugh at the irony. Last month, she was teetering with all four hooves together outside the trailer, not wanting to step in. Now, she was teetering with all four hooves together inside the trailer, not wanting to step off. We walked away from the problem and regrouped. I thought it'd be helpful to build her confidence by backing up everywhere else. I backed her onto a platform and backed off.

Next time, we'll see if she can understand the connection. We'll see if she trusts me enough to say, 'OK, I'll back because I have faith in you.'

TEACH & LEAVE

Folks say you can work with a horse, then leave it be. For weeks. Months. Years, even. As long as you left it in a good place and on good terms, it'll be pretty easy to pick up where you left off.

Horsewoman Kyla Pollard observed that when she revisited a gelding two full years after starting him, with no one riding him in between. "I'm pleased to say he didn't forget too much," said Pollard of the nine year old. "I've had him on fresh cattle, roped off of him, and hit the trails solo. He's well on his way to becoming a great pleasure horse for his owner."

With that in mind, we returned to starting Jodi, the young paint acquired last summer. Over winter, we hadn't done much more than groom her and handle her feet.

Steve brought her back to the round pen with the idea of stirring up as little drama as possible. He saddled her and worked her on the ground without much fuss. Next, he climbed aboard.

I had camera poised and was ready for the fireworks.

She stood for a minute, walked clockwise around the pen a few times, and then switched directions. She was a bit nervous but clearly in a good place.

"She's really come to trust me, so I think at that point my being on her back was almost like 'My pal's up there.' That's how it felt," said Steve.

I was ready for a fun, hats-off, *yee-ha!* moment. What I got was ho hum. I'll take that kind of progress any day.

JODI'S FIRST TRAIL RIDE

Steve has taken his time with Jodi, and it looks like the calm, deliberate approach is paying off.

We headed to Iowa's Pleasant Creek State Park for a long trail ride, just her second ride away from home. As you might expect, the five year old was super curious about everything. Steve gave her time to take in her surroundings. She smelled the ground, investigated sounds, and looked around high and low.

Before we got going, he also asked her to flex her head and neck on both sides, making sure the one-rein stop would be there if he needed it. (A one-rein stop is the way to control your horse's speed and direction by applying steady tension on one rein. Ideally, the horse reacts by flexing its neck and bringing its head toward your stirrup. Many horsemen and women use the one-rein stop as an emergency brake for horses with bolting tendencies. The one-rein stop should always be followed by a quick release when the horse has stopped.)

There's a lot to be said for value of lengthy rides. They give horse and rider a decent chunk of time to work things out, think about things, and most importantly, ride together.

Over eight miles, there were spooks and hazards. But Steve consistently gave her room to move and never nagged her with his reins or legs. The result? This pair got a solid, no-drama ride behind them with Jodi's confidence and willingness firmly intact.

NOTES ON JOLENE

What's the most striking difference between the new mule, Jolene, and her horse herd mates? Not how she moves. Not how she looks. It's how she eats an apple.

When you give Jolene a chunk of apple, she will smell it, take it in her mouth, hold it in her mouth while looking at you, and only then, after a long moment, she will start chewing it.

And so it is. My every intention gets vetted and scrutinized by this guarded new addition. As expected, my skills are being put to the test as I work on helping Jolene become a more confident, more trusting, and more trail-worthy partner.

These past weeks have been dedicated strictly to ground work. Even leading her can be an exercise in patience and consistency. Pressure and release? Better call it light pressure and immediate release.

From previous experience and a few false starts, Jolene knows bolting can get her away from whatever's bothering her. My task, in these early days, is to teach her that bolting means more work and will be less comfortable than just hanging out with me. Round pen work has been effective in getting her to understand I can make her move as well as give her relief.

She moves to a trot easily. No whips or sticks necessary, just pressure with my eyes, arms, and body position. She stops quickly when I relax and stop directing her. She'll let me approach and give her a rub. But she doesn't follow me around like our other horses do. Not yet.

CONFIDENCE – AN INSIDE JOB

How many of us struggle with confidence? How many of us let this struggle impact our horsemanship? These questions hit me full force this summer as I contemplated riding new horses. Sure, I was worried about getting bucked off. But more significantly, I was worried about being worried. Since horses are so darned sensitive, I knew they would feel my insecurity.

Confidence is that vital yet elusive quality affecting many of us in our horsemanship journey. You cannot get it from a tack shop. You cannot get it from working out or taking lessons. Having the gear, knowledge, and experience are all mighty helpful, but confidence is an inside job.

Thankfully, I stumbled upon a few sources of inspiration.

1. A speech by author and artist Neil Gaiman: "Be wise," he told his audience, "and if you cannot be wise, then pretend to be someone wise and behave as they would."

Brilliant! Most people who struggle with confidence think they're just not as good as they actually are. Friends say, "You're holding yourself back!"

So, I pretended to be the Queen of Everything. I pretended to be Miss Horsewoman Extraordinaire.

2. The second inspiration came from Elijah Moore. One day, he told me gently, "I think you'd do better and have more fun if you smiled."

I did. It worked. I hadn't realized how tense I'd gotten. I learned another trick from Steve: when galloping scares you, sing.

Smiling and breathing for humans are not unlike licking lips and chewing for horses: They are physical manifestations of a better mental place.

Sure, I'm playing therapist for a day, but these head games have helped make my first rides with Comet some of the best rides ever. In the process, I've acquired some new horsemanship skills—not roping a cow or tying a special knot—but life skills gained through horse work. I've learned that you're a tense and average rider only if you let yourself be. I've learned that pretending to have fun and ride well often results in real fun and fine riding.

FEEL

Researchers cringe at the term. Horse owners get confused. What is it? And why does it matter?

The journey of understanding feel can last a lifetime. It's easier to grasp if you consider it a large, gradual acquisition of knowledge and not just a definition to memorize. Like learning a new language or having faith in a religion, it takes thoughtfulness and commitment. It's a process full of countless, seemingly mundane moments occasionally interrupted by bright points of epiphany.

Those epiphanies will vault you to the next level of understanding and awareness. Once you have a grasp of it, you'll understand that feel doesn't just apply to horse work. In fact, I learned about feel in horse work through my non-riding sons.

Beau, is a college student and passionate kayaker. He took up the sport six years ago and has since paddled some of the country's most challenging rivers, navigating Class V rapids (the most difficult rank as determined by the International Scale of River Difficulty).

He writes, "As an experienced whitewater boater, I've had the opportunity to be consumed by the river, to feel tiny amongst massive forces...I attribute my success to working with the river and not against it.

"To be tuned to react to any ripple in the eddy line, to use re-circulating waves to control my speed, and to know where to plant my paddle blade are lessons taught by the river, not by humans.

"What I have with the river is not so much a friendship but a bond like a child has to a parent...It offers countless lessons. As long as you let it teach you."

Beau's river is my horse.

More than any book, DVD, or real-live clinician, my own observations of horses' responses and initiatives have helped improve my horsemanship. Sometimes I'll just sit and watch them move and communicate with each other. Sometimes in the saddle, I'll close my eyes to better feel their movement.

Aidan, Beau's older brother, has excelled at soccer. He was the defensive anchor on a college team that twice advanced in the NCAA tournament. His attitude toward games parallels how I approach trail rides. From the outsider's perspective, it looks like just another day. But it's a unique, collective experience.

He writes, "Playing soccer is like taking part in a painting that paints itself. You have a role in the outcome of the painting, but you alone don't paint the painting. Every game produces a new painting, a different painting, one with different strokes, composition, and subject matter.

"Though the game is confined to a certain space, no matter how many games you play, each time you play, the ball—and you—follow a different path, a different trajectory. You never get tired of painting, even though you're playing the same game."

Feel, then, is an awareness of action and reaction. It's an understanding that your thoughts, behaviors, and movements have an impact on your horse. But feel is also an awareness of your horse's actions and behaviors. Feel is the product of the horse-rider connection.

Why does feel matter? Once you embrace the idea of feel, you can become quieter and more effective in your cues.

Great horsemen and women don't get amazing results because their horses are specially trained. They impress because they notice things we don't. They react to messages we haven't even seen or heard. They have more responsive horses because they themselves are more responsive.

For a new soccer, kayak, or riding fan, lots of important developments will go completely unnoticed. That's why the uninformed think certain sports are so 'boring.' Or as horseman Mike Kevil noted, "Watching a colt starting can be a little like watching paint dry."

Was there a time in your life when you didn't know what ear pinning meant? Did you always know that lip-licking was a 'pressure's off' reaction? Can you now sense each individual hoof fall when you ride?

Time with horses, awareness, and experience will teach you these things if you let them. And as you develop, actions and reactions will become less conscious efforts.

Defined without ruler, stopwatch, or scale, it's no wonder so many masters struggle to define feel. How do you quantify a process, full of tiny split-second movements and choices? In any given minute, there might be a dozen horse-human interactions. Some are deliberate. Some are subconscious. Some are unwitting.

Or, as Aidan writes, "When I play soccer, I don't feel like I am the one who is playing. My body knows much better where to pass, where to run, where to situate myself, when to tackle (and when not to) than I do. Before I even have the chance to think, my body is already acting. Hence the painting that paints itself."

MULTITASKING AS AWARENESS

There's a lot of research out there that disparages multitasking. Scientists say it's inefficient. They say ideal productivity and efficiency requires focus. But often horse handling requires a certain lack of focus and an ability to take in, understand, and react to multiple developments, all at the same time. The key, of course is awareness.

Consider working with a horse in a paddock with other horses. As you approach a horse for haltering, you must assess:

- His temperament
- His location and relationship compared to the other horses (like whether he likes to screen himself or whether he gets bullied)
- How hungry he may be
- How bothered by bugs he may be

As you halter and move your horse, a whole new set of tasks appear:

- How does he move through gates?
- Will the others want to come too?
- How well does that gate close?

You answer these questions by:

- Watching ears and lips and tails
- Watching for bracing or willingness
- Listening for movement that you might not see
- Being aware of the environmental conditions (like an approaching storm or slippery surfaces)

Our work is not unlike that of an office manager or stay-at-home parent. On any given moment, working with horses requires us to be all there, but it may not require us to focus on just one thing. If we were to focus on just haltering a horse, we might end up hurt or the horse might get loose. The wider lens often serves us better.

BOLTING & RIDER FEAR

Dr. Sue McDonnell is the founding head of the Equine Behavior Program at the University of Pennsylvania and a certified Applied Animal Behaviorist. She's a big deal at a big university with a stellar reputation for producing equine vets. So it was dismaying to read her post in the Behavior Q & A section of TheHorse.com. McDonnell was asked about the prospects for rehabbing an ex-racehorse from his bolting tendencies. Her paraphrased response:

- Bolting is a near-impossible habit to break and many trainers simply give up on horses "with this kind of behavior."
- That said, it might help to develop a more trusting, positive relationship with the horse so that when he goes to bolt, he might stay with you instead.

- I've only ever known of one horse that's overcome a bolting tendency. It was a miracle turnaround.

But in knowing the horse's instinctual needs and reviewing top clinicians, we know:

- To bolt is to be a horse. Horses are prey animals and when they get scared, flight is their auto-response.
- Horses NEED to have that fifth gear. They need to have a rider aboard who can let them move fast and not keep them constrained when they panic.
- Solving the bolting issue has almost nothing to do with a warm and fuzzy relationship. It has everything to do with training—namely, lateral flexion and the one-rein stop. (Lateral flexion is the horse's head and neck movement from facing forward to bending toward its side or toward the rider's shin if there is a rider aboard. This is a trained movement essential for one-rein stops.)

In the opening clip of *7 Clinics* with Buck Brannaman, the protégé of Ray Hunt talks about rider fear. "Fear is a big thing that just owns some people. It can be overwhelming," he said.

But instead of giving up on their horses, Brannaman implores his students to work with them at full speed and to learn how to use flexion and the one-rein stop. "You do need to get a horse to where you can open him up and go. You gotta have the right kind of footing. A horse is pretty incomplete if you can't just open him up and not have him lose his mind...

"I just practice dialing it up, dialing it back down, dialing it up, dialing it back down, and getting them quiet again...I go like I've got a job. So he's not scared to move out...Set yourself up for success.

"You practice those things. You need to know you can."

In the DVD, a woman is working in a round pen. Her horse starts to panic. His spinning turns into racing, and around the pen he goes. The woman never pulls on the reins but allows him to churn away. When he starts slowing, she strokes his neck. When he stops, she loves on him.

When Steve works on lateral flexion with his horse, Jodi, by simply learning to bend with his gentle contact, Jodi will accept a one-rein stop later on as the training evolves.

Brannaman on flexion and the one-rein stop: "In order for you to advance, you have to do this without a problem. This will be absolutely necessary for you to do...If you can't walk, trot, and canter and then stop with a one-rein stop, then you ought to practice every chance you get....It ought to be something that you would bet your life on."

You need the skill and confidence NOT to constrain a horse when it bolts or panics.

As Martin Black wrote in *Evidence-Based Horsemanship*, "By pulling on the head, we make horses feel they can't get away, which causes more panic. In some situations, horses may need only a short distance to feel safe, but when [constraint] follows them, they continue their fight for freedom."

McDonnell was right when she told readers that matters will get worse only when the rider feels afraid or insecure. But it's the fear, not the horse they need to rein in.

Do you have a horse who likes to bolt? How often do you gallop with him? How often do you let him move when something frightens him?

As one horse owner said, "A horse was never running off with me, as long as I was riding right along with it."

Knowledge and practice, in the form of one-rein stops and flexion, will save the horse and the partnership.

Bolting – Sidebar I

My name is Maddy and I own a bolting horse. The first time we met, she tossed me. The second time, she tossed me too. I love her dearly, but after those experiences, I stopped riding her. For several months, she was the one left behind.

This mare—so full of life, so willing to go—was another one of those supposed 'lost causes.'

Then I got help. Steve suggested I direct her instead of pulling back on both reins. So simple. But resisting the impulse to restrain-through-reins is harder than it sounds. It involves detangling muscle-memory and mental habits long ingrained over years of novice riding.

After reading *The Power of Habit* by Charles Duhigg, I know why it's so hard. You literally have to bypass old neural pathways and create new ones in your brain.

While my horse's auto-response to anything peripherally scary was movement, my response to her response was constraint. This had to stop.

I learned to relax and hold on. I learned to steer instead of trying to shut her down. We connected. My cues and our rapport got good enough for us to move from a snaffle to a bosal. (A snaffle is any metal bit with a single joint in the middle and with various designs of rings on which to attach the reins. A bosal is a rawhide noseband with a leather hanger running from it over the poll; it allows horse and rider to have a more sensitive connection than with a snaffle.)

As I so often realize, the problem was with me, not her. I needed more skill and more confidence to go with it. (Again, simpler than it sounds.)

My name is Maddy. And I'm getting better.

Bolting – Sidebar II

The woman in Craig Cameron's clinic was pulling on the reins too much. Cameron smiled and yelled, "Let go! Where's he gonna go? You're in an arena!"

His thought, I presume, was that we're safer in an arena if the horse ends up doing something unsafe, like bucking or bolting.

But a recent ride with my pony, Pep, taught me that wide open spaces can be exhilarating AND safe too. Pep is another one with a strong distaste for rein contact. She's tossed me a few times when I wanted her to stop and did so with too much rein contact. But I've learned to let her go. If she wants to move, I let her. But I get to direct where she's going.

At the beach for the first time, she had no interest in standing still or even walking, so I directed her in big, quick circles. Then we did small, quick circles. There were no fences to hit. No trees to duck. No rocks or holes to dodge. Within ten minutes, she was walking and stopping with hardly any rein contact. She felt better. I felt better.

BREAKING BAD AND HORSE SUCCESS

Peter Gould, a writer and producer for *Breaking Bad*, one of the most successful and critically-acclaimed TV series ever, was talking about the process of writing episodes and how he considers and respects the audience.

"Let them be smart," Gould said. "As Billy Wilder said, 'Give them two and two. Let them make four. They'll love you forever.'"

In other words, let the story be a collaboration, not a mandate. Not a bad strategy for horsemanship, either.

SIX:

Interviews &
Conversations

THE WISDOM OF BILL & TOM DORRANCE

When we consider improvements to horsemanship, the wisdom of Bill and Tom Dorrance resonates powerfully and universally across all disciplines. For the Dorrances, it wasn't about English or Western, dressage or reining. It was about getting with the horse.

What you might learn from the Dorrances was a "manner of learning whose subject was nominally the horse but that extended itself in surprising directions to include dogs, cattle, and people," wrote Verlyn Klinkenborg in the *New York Times*.

Their techniques were rooted in observation and humility.

Bill Dorrance passed away in 1999; Tom died in 2003. Only a handful of men and women got to spend considerable time with these Oregon-born California men. For these protégés, the Dorrance years were lifealtering.

Shouldn't these student memories be celebrated and recorded for posterity? That was the plea I brought to the folks at *Western Folklife* in the middle of 2013. *Western Folklife* puts on the National Cowboy Poetry Gathering, an eclectic exposition of cowboy lore and artistry. What better place to present a Dorrance remembrance? Over several months, *Western Folklife* put the pieces of this idea together, creating a format and inviting guests.

On a snowy January day in the G Three Bar Theater, four men and one woman shared their treasured memories to a standing-room-only crowd. Over the ninety-minute session, it became clear the Dorrances weren't just interested in making them better with horses. They wanted them to be better at life too.

The participants:

Randy Rieman—colt-starter, clinician, rawhide braider, and cowboy poetry reciter

Ellen Eckstein—international dressage rider based in Templeton, California, who studied for many years with Tom

Bryan Neubert—well-known clinician who lived near the Dorrances in Salinas, California, and worked for years with them

Thomas Petit Marvel—cowboy-turned-pilot who worked nearby on the 25 Ranch and as a young cowboy knew the Dorrances

Mike Beck—horseman and singer-songwriter who's shared Bill's insights internationally, especially in Scandinavia

Here are excerpted highlights from the Dorrance roundtable, published with permission from *Western Folklife*:

Mike Beck

Bill got me to start to see things, to observe things and to slow down. I was just in a hurry about everything. There were so many things he would observe.

We'd go to town for groceries. He'd have me drive his '65 Impala to Star Market. He'd have me park near the sidewalk and I was trying to figure out why…I'd come back and he'd say, you know that one feller, the way he moved down the street, he'd look pretty good on a horse. And I thought, my god, when does he ever quit thinking about it? He liked to get you interested…He started to let me see that there was nothing ordinary at all.

Some time later, I went back out with Bryan. I remember, I said, "Boy, there's a lot of bluebirds this year. There's a lot of water in this draw. There's so many big bucks this year."

Bryan said, 'Hell, they were all here last year.'

So he set me off on a course of trying to see the special thing in every horse. I can't begin to thank him enough for how he changed my life in a beautiful way.

Bryan Neubert

I met Bill's boys in high school. I really wanted to find somebody to help me with horse work…I didn't know he knew a thing about horses…He was just another rancher.

But I go in the tack room there and he's got a Champion Bridle Horse saddle there and he's got a Champion Hackamore Horse saddle there too. For Salinas. Salinas is a big one.

I said, "Have you ever shown horses? Did you win these?"

Yeh.

I don't really want to go into how he changed my life. This isn't about me. But I have no idea where I would have been or what I would have done if I hadn't have met them… It totally changed things. He was the most sensitive, nicest person I'd ever met.

❦ – ❧

All the presenters recalled the memory and genius of the Dorrance brothers. Here, Randy Rieman recalls a moment with Tom.

Randy Rieman

It was five years after his eightieth birthday party and he met a man. He said, "I believe I do remember you. You were at my eightieth birthday party."

There were thirty or forty horses and people at this clinic to celebrate his eightieth birthday…The guy was just amazed that Tom remembered.

"Yeah, I think you had a two-year-old sorrel filly," said Tom.

And the guy said, 'Yeah. I did.'

And Tom said, "But you didn't own that horse. A woman from Washington owned that horse."

And he said, 'That's right.'

And Tom said, "And you're a horseshoer from Washington, aren't you?"

And the guy said, 'Yeah. I am.'

That was an example of Tom's memory.

∽ – ∝

Bryan recalled Tom's memory, too, when they were working in Hollister, California, in the 60s. They were responsible for nineteen horses and each was riding several per day.

Bryan Neubert

Tom would say, 'How's that horse feel?'

I'd say, "Pretty good."

Tom would say, 'Remember, you rode that horse last Wednesday when we gathered the bulls. And you rode him the Thursday before when we were down checking the cattle. And you rode him Friday before that.'

And he talked about how that horse was progressing all through those rides. I mean, a lot of times I can't remember what I had for breakfast. He talked about the importance of your progress and in your ability to remember and observe and compare. And he darn sure had that.

Bryan continues: Ray Hunt got Tom to go to Bozeman to do a clinic. There was a woman there. He said, "I've seen you before." He didn't say he'd met her.

She said, 'I don't believe so.'

He said, "Let me sleep on it."

The next day, he said to her, "Could you have been in a beauty contest that would have been on national television?"

She said, 'Well, I was Miss Montana in the Miss America contest ten years ago.'

And he said, "That's where I've seen you."

Before I knew him, I would contest his memory. I'd go on weekends and just take a horse or two…He'd say, 'I guess it's been seven weeks since you were here last?'

I'd say, "I don't think it's been that long." Like, if I had known him better, I would never say that.

He said, 'Well, let's figure it out:

'Last weekend, I stayed home.

'Weekend before that we went to town.

'Weekend before that I went up to Bill's.

'Weekend before that I stayed home.

'Weekend before that I stayed home.

'Weekend before that so-and-so came.

'Weekend before that you were here.'

I said, "I guess it has been seven weeks."

Incredible memory.

Randy

Tom and Bill were alike in so many ways but they were really different too…If you asked Tom something, he would answer with something like 'The oxen is slow but the earth is patient.' It was so vague. If you asked Bill the same question, he would say, 'Put your left foot here and take your right hand…' It was so different.

But here's a way they were similar:

We were braiding in Bill's rawhide room, and Margaret, Tom's wife, was riding around the barnyard. And we're in there braiding. Bill's got his head down. I've got my head down.

We hear this big splat out in the barnyard and without looking up, Bill says, "Sounds like Margaret's come off her horse."

Total calm, like, 'Did you want decaf?'

I peek out there and sure enough, Margaret was on the ground, in pain. So Bill grabbed his cane and off we went. Bill says, "Did your horse get out from under you, Margaret?"

'Yes.' (Here, Randy grits his teeth.)

"Are you OK?" asks Bill.

'I think I broke my hip.'

"Can you move your legs?" asks Bill.

'Yes.' (more gritted teeth)

"You're all right."

So she says, 'No. I'm not. You git Tom.'

So, Tom pulled up on his golf cart and he says, "Did your horse get out from under you?"

'Yes.'

"Are you all right?"

'I think I broke my hip.'

And Tom said, "Can you move your legs?"

'Yes.'

He said, "You're all right."

Randy continues:

I was thinking, aside from just being brilliant and passionate about horses what really set these guys apart was they had such a non-adversarial approach and they had incredible compassion for the horse and the people.

They weren't on a time clock. Ever. You stopped when there was a good opportunity and you continued until there was a good opportunity.

At a clinic, Bill was trying to help this young feller... He was starting to heat up and the horse was starting to heat up. It got pretty warm.

Super frustrated, he just looked at Bill and he said, "How long is this supposed to take?" Bill chuckled and said, 'I don't know about you, but I got from now on.'

Ellen Eckstein

Many people don't know it, but Tom was a show-off. I was having trouble with flying changes. He would get on my horse and do flying changes... He literally put the reins over his neck, folded his arms and he was cantering around with this horse, doing flying changes every couple of strides on this horse that I couldn't do flying changes on.

He rode over and said, 'You can go to town and back between strides with that horse,' he said. 'That's what you want.'

It was wonderful.

Bryan

Tom just did not spend money. I saw that he resoled boots with tires. He'd used a grinder and all the nail holes had been counter sunk.

Once someone asked him what kind of boots he liked.

He said, 'I have a strict criteria I follow when I pick out boots.'

What's that?

'Cheapest ones on the rack.'

Mike Beck

In a lot of ways, Bill was setting me up just the way he was setting up his horses. There was no difference between them. I'd leave and as soon as I got out the gate, the first thing I was thinking about was 'when do I get to go back?' It was a good feeling that I got up there.

Randy

Randy talks about his getting a job starting colts at the Parker Ranch in Hawaii, one of the biggest ranches in the country. "I had a chance to go ride some colts out at this place. The feller didn't know me so he was trying to call a couple references. So I used Bryan Neubert and Bill Dorrance.

"The feller asked Bill if I could get the job done. And Bill told him, 'Yeah, he'd probably get the job done.'

That was his reference.

The next day Bill said, 'Feller called here wanting to know if you could do the job. I was kinda tempted to tell him 'no' because I'm gonna lose my rawhide partner.'

Bill's rawhide room was a treasure house and I just loved being in there.

Randy on Reata Braiding

I was so proud to get to braiding these reatas. I wanted to give one to Bill to say thank you for teaching me. This reata was ninety feet. I'd worked real hard on it.

If you know anything about a reata…it's four strands of rawhide. Each strand is about a quarter-inch wide. Every quarter inch, there's a cross…Over ninety-two feet, there's quarter-inch crosses.

I handed it to Bill.

In ten seconds, he said, 'I see you turned a strand over here.'

See, there are two sides, a flesh side and a hair side, and they are hard to distinguish. In ten seconds, over ninety feet of rope, he spotted that one spot. It stuck out like somebody's thumb.

Ellen

I learned about balance and straightness from Tom. Every time I had a problem with a horse, it went back to balance and straightness. It went from the outside of the horse all the way to the inside of the horse. It went back to the horse's sense of self-preservation. Tom would say that if a horse is off balance, it scares him. Then you get your bucking and rearing.

Most problem horses are problem horses because of lack of balance or straightness…They feel they can't handle themselves. It wasn't so difficult then to fix them because of knowing that.

Tom Marvel

The one thing I wanted to impart on everyone here is the influences the Dorrances have had on my life, over my lifetime. It's made me a far better person. I not only learned a better feel with horses. I was an aviator. And I learned the feel of airplanes, learned the feel with people. I was tremendously lucky and proud that I got to know and work with the Dorrances.

Randy

It's pretty obvious how much we adored these men and how much they did for us, inside and out.

\ – \

At the round table conclusion, Randy Rieman read a letter from Margaret Dorrance. It reads in part:

> It's been eleven years since Tom passed and although he's gone physically I think a lot of us still feel his presence in our lives. He never set out to change the world but he sure made a lot of difference to a lot of people in their lives and of course in the lives of many horses.
>
> I always thought he was something special but then that's why I married him. But seriously, I never thought he would make such an impact either. He was just being himself, which I think is part of the reason he's had such an impact in the horse world. Even though he had such

great success at understanding what the horse thought and reacted to things, Tom was always searching for a better way.

Always.

So was Bill.

If today he was successful in something with the horse, then tomorrow he was thinking about how he might make that easier or better for the horse. He was constantly searching and working things out and that was one of the reasons I think he was so extraordinary.

BEN MASTERS – *UNBRANDED*

A few years ago, Ben Masters took a two-thousand-mile backcountry adventure from Santa Fe, New Mexico, to the Canadian border. Now, the Texas A & M graduate has masterminded *Unbranded*, the documentary film in-the-making of four friends, fourteen BLM mustangs, and a BLM burro as they travel from the Mexican to the Canadian borders.

I interviewed Masters as the group rode just over halfway of their three-thousand-mile journey.

Maddy Butcher Gray (MBG): You did an immense amount of planning. Are things going as you imagined?

Masters: There are so many variables that are outside of your control that you can't really anticipate a lot of the things that are going to happen to you. So I don't try to imagine what it's going to be like....But I've been absolutely blown away by the scenery we've gone through. Arizona. I had absolutely no idea that the Southwest, especially that desert country, could be so beautiful in the spring or summer time. That's been my biggest shock just how neat the scenery has been and also the lack of people.

MBG: How often to you see other people?

Masters: Depends on our location. If we're in the backcountry, it may be two or three days before we see anyone. But we have to move from one national forest to another national forest, we may see a hundred people if we're going through town or whatever. On our route, we generally avoid them, but it's nice to drop down into town and get something to eat every once in a while.

MBG: Your journey will be a film documentary. How often do you have other people with you?

Masters: We have a cameraman with us about 80 percent of the time. There are two cameramen. They alternate out: Cameraman 1 for ten days. Then Cameraman 2 for ten days. Then we'll have a week off with no cameraman. It goes through cycles. That way, they can stay fresh. They can stay energized. Running all over the mountains getting footage is a real task.

MBG: And how many animals are you working with?

Masters: We have fourteen horses and a donkey. We have four pack horses and five saddle horses. The remainder are loose. They are just following behind. So, they're getting a day off. We rotate through.

MBG: How many miles are you doing and do your horses have shoes?

Masters: We ride approximately twenty miles a day. Yes, we have to have shoes. If they were barefoot, our horses would make it maybe three hundred to four hundred miles before they completely wore through their hooves. They cannot do this without shoes.

MBG: Can all of you put on and take off shoes if you need to?

Masters: We can, but we aren't professionals. So we try to get a professional shoer to come out and do it for us whenever we need to if possible. We can do it, but I don't want to risk our horses' feet if I can get a professional to do it.

MBG: Twenty miles is a lot of work. Do you have to supplement grazing with any grain?

Masters: We do give them grain…Not as often as I'd like. We try to pack some with us…That also helps keep them close to camp if there's food around. We give them about five pounds of grain every other day. Not really enough, but it's the maximum amount we can take with us. It weighs a lot.

MBG: How are horses holding up?

Masters: They are trim. They are in marathon shape. They are in unbelievable shape. We'll climb a hill that's a thousand feet elevation, and they don't even break into a sweat.

$$\approx - \ll$$

Our interview with *Unbranded*'s Masters continues as they head into Yellowstone National Park:

MBG: We've noticed Unbranded has a strong message of conservation and public open space.

Masters: Yeah, absolutely. There's 773 million acres of public space in the United States, and I don't think a lot of people realize it's there and ours to use. So, almost our entire route, from Mexico to Canada, is a patchwork of BLM, national forests, national parks, wilderness areas. I think it's pretty incredible that there's a corridor of public land with almost no fences all the way from Mexico to Canada that you can still do a trip like this on.

MBG: I noticed you all are carrying guns? Is that for grizzlies or something else?

Masters: That's to kill a horse if it breaks a leg.

MBG: Have you ever had to do that?

Masters: No. Hopefully, we'll never have to pull those pistol triggers.

MBG: You already have a strong fan base. Have there been any liabilities associated with the advanced promotion?

Masters: No, we haven't had any crazy stalkers come out to try to hunt us down or anything like that. We haven't had any negatives. Only positives.

MBG: You took a similar trip with two friends in 2010. Can you tell me a bit about it?

Masters: We started with six horses. The common theme with that trip is that the mustangs outperformed the quarter horses. We had to replenish the quarter horses, whereas the mustangs went the entire way. That's why we're trying to use mustangs this trip. It took four and a half months, and it loosely followed the Continental Divide from Santa Fe to the Canadian border.

MBG: You often mention nice meals when you occasionally reach towns. How are you hanging in there with camp meals?

Masters: We re-supply food every ten days or so. Before the trip started, we prepackaged food boxes that had everything we needed, and then our mothers sent us those food packages so we could pick them up. That way we would not have to go shopping.

MBG: What's a typical day's menu?

Masters: We eat trail mix bars and candy and that kind of thing all day, and then we just have one big dinner. Usually, it consists of pasta and canned foods and then we have some dried foods, too. Astronaut food kind of stuff.

MBG: How about jerky?

Masters: We eat a lot of jerky.

MBG: It sounds similar to backpacking.

Masters: Exactly.

MBG: You're heading out of cellular phone service now?

Masters: Correct. We're about to go through the Teton Wilderness, Yellowstone Park, Gallatin National Forest, Beaverhead-Deerlodge National Forest. We'll be out of cell phone range until August.

MBG: So, if something bad happens, what's your contingency plan?

Masters: We have a satellite phone, and we also have an emergency beacon where you hit the red button and a helicopter comes in and brings you out.

MBG: I was studying the route and your time and mileage. The route planning seems like an incredible logistical feat.

Masters: Thank you.

MBG: I imagine it took a lot of time.

Masters: You have no idea. There are so many things to take into consideration: The elevation, the time of year, the grade and condition of the elevation at that time of the year, water availability. There's a lot of thought that went into planning the route. Realistically, it took about a year or so. I don't know how many hundreds of hours. It paid off. The route's been good to us. We haven't had too many mishaps.

ॐ – ॐ

Our interview with *Unbranded*'s Ben Masters continues as the team heads north from Yellowstone:

MBG: Looking ahead, how does your route look?

Masters: It's going to be great. This is the jewel of the trip right here. It's the deepest backcountry in the lower forty-eight. Probably three hundred miles, and you cross only two or three roads. But there's a lot of buffalo up here, bears and wolves, a few more of the larger animals.

MBG: Are you concerned that the horses would be attacked?

Masters: It's not so much that they'd attack us, but the horses get really frightened from stuff like that. Moose and that kind of thing scare your horses. I think we're well prepared for it. If anything does happen, we have an escape route and satellite phone...But I think we'll be just fine.

MBG: There's such a contrast between that 'being in wilderness' state of mind, and then what you'll encounter when you finish the trip, with the documentary production, marketing, appearances, and all that. It will be a bit of a culture shock, won't it?

Masters: Yeah, I didn't really think that one all the way through (laughing). I don't think any of us wanted to make the film to do anything but make a conservation message and to try to promote the adoption of these wild horses. You're right. It's going to be a hassle, being in the spotlight sometimes. But I think we have the ability to make a powerful message about conservation of open spaces and the adoption of mustangs.

There's not enough room out there for them. And sometimes I feel like there's not a lot of room out there for us, either. I think we're saving each other by doing this long trip. We're getting them out of their captivity, and they're helping us get out of ours.

UNBRANDED – Sidebar

Recently, I headed to Montana to ride with Ben Masters, the team leader of *Unbranded*. We took two of his mustangs south of Bozeman into the Gallatin National Forest for a beautiful ride through the season's first several inches of snow. I rode Dinosaur, a palomino gelding from Utah. Masters rode Chief, a good-looking grey gelding.

We climbed from about six thousand feet elevation at the trail head to seven thousand on snowy paths abutting Ted Turner's massive Flying D Ranch. (The Flying D covers over one hundred thirteen thousand acres. All told, Turner owns over two million acres, making him the second largest individual landowner in North America.)

Did I mention a fear of heights? At times, the trail left little room for error. But I knew better than to try to guide Dino. In fact, he did just fine with little or no rein contact. Sketchy bridges, sheer drop-offs, icy spots: He did marvelously on all.

Sure-footed, for sure. The horses were in impressive condition, even after several weeks off. We climbed for more than an hour, never stopping. Dino wasn't even breathing hard.

For these guys, the day was inconsequential, compared to what the two horses and one Texan have seen this year.

But the ride and the good company were a treat for me.

FERGUS!

The wise, white-faced goofball has inspired more laughs and devotion than any cartoon horse in recent memory.

Fergus is the creation of Jean Abernethy, a petite, fifty-two-year-old Canadian. The Ontario College of Art graduate is also an accomplished artist of more serious work, a book illustrator, an experienced commercial artist, and of course, a horsewoman.

Abernethy, who grew up on a farm north of Toronto, remains humble about her Fergus success. Everyone appreciates the funny moments of horse ownership, she said, "I just happen to be someone who can draw."

While Fergus may be silly, Abernethy connects with fans because she understands horses from an informed perspective. She has a wealth of barn and trail experience, and she's taken collegiate courses in equine science and management. She's even built her own saddle.

MBG: Is Fergus a horse from your past, a mix of several horses, or one from your imagination?

JA: I like to say Fergus is a little bit of every horse I've ever met. There is no particular one horse. Although when I was thirteen years old, my father let me buy a colt off a PMU farm. I had outgrown the family pony. It was in the fall. He was a weanling. That horse had a lot of white on his face. That's where Fergus's white face came from. His name was Justin. That was an incredible horse. He was a quarter horse crossed with we don't know what. Perhaps Standardbred. He was 15-2. An all around great guy.

MBG: Did Justin teach you or did you teach Justin?

JA: Yes. He taught me a lot. I thought I was teaching him. But you know how it is. It's mutual. He taught me a lot about forgiveness. Because I thought I knew what I was doing. He suffered because of it. He was amazing. He forgave a lot of childish mistakes. I was thirteen, after all. I had learned a lot from the family pony. I started riding her at the age of seven. She was tiny and very, very skittish. And we had everything for her to spook at—pigs, dogs, you name it. There was no saddle. So, by the time I got to the horse, I was strong and I could ride."

MBG: Fergus has had such wonderful success on Facebook. Why do you think he's been so well received?

JA: I attribute the success to the humor being right where horse people's hearts are. Some of these comics have been around a while.

Some have been around before Facebook existed. We started in black and white—pen, brush, paper. I'm getting some of them out of the mothballs. I'm coloring them on the computer, and now I can show them to the whole world. Not just magazines. The response is terrific.

MBG: How does an average Fergus moment happen? How does it evolve to a finished piece?

JA: Usually, it happens in the barn. Some of them are kind of philosophical. They don't evolve in any time at all. But the wild turkey on the trail; what can you do but laugh? Or the Clydesdale that stands on your foot? That just happened… and I just happen to be able to draw pictures of it and then make the horses look goofy.

MBG: How long does it take?

JA: One of those comic strips is about four hours. At least.

MBG: You're an accomplished artist, aside from Fergus. What else are you up to?

JA: Fergus is taking up about half my time lately. I'm also working on illustrating a book for an author in Australia. I have some advertising work. I have the Sweet Pea character for Sweet PDZ, the horse stall refresher product. It's a little character I invented for them. We've had some fun with her.

MBG: Do you have a business strategy?

JA: Business strategy? Honey, you're talking to an artist! That's very hard thing for creative people.

MBG: Your 'Life is Short' line has had a lot of notice.

JA: Yes, I think it's because a lot of people in the horse industry are women of our age. You know how it is. You hit the middle age of your life, and life starts to look pretty short. And you start to look at what's really important. And that's why that design goes right to the core of where our hearts are.

MBG: How did you name Fergus?

156

JA: My grandfather's Christian name was Ferguson. I suppose it probably comes from that more than anything else. I wanted a name with a "U" in it because the horseshoe fits in there so perfectly. It's part of my Scotch-Irish heritage. That and my grandfather's name…It all fit together. Seems to work.

MBG: Sure does.

LESLIE DESMOND

Fifteen years ago, Leslie Desmond wrote the popular *True Horsemanship through Feel* with the late and legendary Bill Dorrance.

MBG: Scientists and people who need to define things literally struggle to define feel.

LD: As they have struggled for millennia to define the concept of love. There are certain things that maybe you can't put in a box. And maybe that might be one of them. But you know it when you see it, and you know it when you feel it. And that's part of the gift that the horse has for us, is that that horse can take you through a door that no one has ever opened for you.

MBG: When someone asks you to define feel, what do you say?

LD: I would say that I spent four and a half years watching Bill Dorrance struggle with the same definition, which he wanted to commit to paper. In the end, he divided it into six aspects out of a multitude of other options. He got it very well defined for his own purposes. But I would just take an approach like this and say: If you can understand the difference between the way that you would remove with your finger an eyelash from the face of an infant versus what it would require of you to knock a fencepost down through some permafrost…If you can really understand the difference and the variations in those applications of feel, then you've got enough to proceed. OK?

If you, for example, can't taste the difference between a habanero and vanilla ice cream, then we'll have to go to another example. OK? If you want to go to Houston in August and step out of an air-conditioned plane and can't feel the difference, then we'll have to keep looking for whatever aspect of feel you do understand.

Most people are going to be able to know either with sight, sound, touch or smell…to have some measurable response. They're going to know that they are having a different experience of those things. All of those are variations on feel. But the feel I'm interested in teaching people is the feel of release.

MBG: With the advance of technology and all the possibilities that are out there to communicate on a technological level, do you find your students more in touch with you or less in touch with you?

LD: It's far better.

MBG: Is that because they relish the opportunity for a real experience? What do you attribute it to?

LD: Television and the Internet. Because everything except what I'm doing is out there, and in multiples. By the time someone's really talking to me seriously, they know what they want. I think by the time they pick up the phone and call me, they're sure that they're unsure about what to do next.

DAHLOV IPCAR

Over her ninety-six years, Dahlov Ipcar has produced an immense feast of fanciful paintings and illustrations. She started young and by age twenty-one, had her own solo exhibit at the Museum of Modern Art in New York City. She's written scores of books and created impressive works of fabric, hooked rug, and needlepoint.

"[She] anchors one of the outer boundaries of Maine's rich and varied world of the visual arts. She nourishes the notion that Maine art is not provincial, narrow or predictable," gallery owner and artist Tom Crotty told the *New Maine Times*.

For much of her life, she's lived simply in Georgetown, Maine, choosing the coastal town over New York City, where she spent her early school years. She chose the slow lane, for sure, working a farm with her husband Adolf. They reared two sons, raised animals, and grew vegetables. Earlier this year, Georgetown bestowed her with its Outstanding Citizen Award.

We spoke with this amazing woman at her home where she expounded on her affinity for horses, her work habits, and more.

MBG: How did you come to know horses?

Ipcar: When I was ten, my parents rented a pony for the summer. I had a girlfriend. We just took turns riding the pony. Nobody would give us any instruction. We just rode.

When I was eleven, they decided to give me riding lessons in Central Park, and that's where I really learned to ride, to use the reins, and all that. And then my mother bought me a horse. It was not the best saddle horse in the world. It was a good horse. It had been trained as a harness racer, and I drove it in a buggy, and I rode it and I drove it in a hay rake. Whenever you turned the corner in the hay rake, there was a sound that he'd think was the beginning of the race. It'd go BANG!

MBG: He came off a Maine track?

Ipcar: Yes. He was an unsuccessful racer. He did pretty well going down the road with me. Once there was a car following behind us, and they said, 'Gee! That horse can really go! He went thirty-five miles per hour!' I still had the horse when I got married at eighteen…We had a workhorse, a great big Percheron. Adolf used to ride the workhorse, and I'd ride the saddle horse. We went around. There were all kinds of abandoned houses and small roads around these woods around here.

MBG: You taught yourself?

Ipcar: Yes, I had basic instruction. I spent a lot of time polishing harnesses, which nobody had ever done around this place. My friend gave me a book, *Advanced Equitation.* She thought we were beyond basic equitation. She thought that was too low brow. But we certainly weren't up to advanced.

MBG: Did you continue to have horses as an adult?

Ipcar: We bought a pony for our kids. She was kind of a mean little thing. Ponies get spoiled because nobody really rides them except children who don't know how to control them, and she'd go in the frog pond and lie down and roll with the saddle on and try to knock the kids off under branches. We kept a horse for the winter. He was called Hi Boy. He was like a giraffe. He had to spread his legs to eat. His legs were much longer than his neck.

MBG: You paint so many animals, including horses. Is that your preference?

Ipcar: I seem to draw on the connection of all animals. I can almost draw animals without thinking even. I have trouble with people. Fairly recently, they [researchers] admitted that animals have emotions. They always said they were clockwork, you know, they went by instinct and were programmed, which is nonsense. All you have to do is have an animal, you know it. It has just as much brain power, not quite as much as you but plenty in other ways.

Ipcar: [to her cat, Grendel]: What do you say, baby? Isn't that true?

MBG: Tell me about your riding days.

Ipcar: I would say it was the only outdoor sport I enjoyed. I enjoyed having a horse and riding. We also swam a lot, but I never took to boats, and I never took to any of this baseball or any of the regular sports. Chess and horses were the only sports I ever enjoyed.

Riding here, you run out of interesting trails very rapidly. You'd like to go further. But I never got real journeys with horses. To get to Brunswick was about as far as I ever got. We always got to Bath. We always had to cross [the Kennebec River, which is nearly a mile wide in Bath]. We started on ferries. I can't remember taking the horse on ferries, but we must have because we had to take the horse to the blacksmith. The blacksmith was in Brunswick. They didn't come to you in those days.

...There were several bridges. There were cars on the roads and the roads weren't as wide. But people were a little more aware of horses. I think a lot of people still had horses when we first came here. There were a lot of people who drove horses in buggies.

MBG: Have you always been interested in painting horses?

Ipcar: Off and on through my life. I do a horse picture when I feel inspired to do a horse picture. I don't quite know why. There was something fashionable about being an artist who did horses, and I resisted that, though I've done some nice racehorse pictures. We used to go to the fairs, my mother and I. My husband and I. I did a lot of sketching of stables and made some nice pictures with the pageantry of it. The Topsham Fair was held in October then...Now it's held in August to get the tourists, but it lacks something when it's not a harvest fair.

MBG: What medium do you use? How do you get started?

Ipcar: I work with lots of sketches and sketchbooks. I use these often with oil paintings. My mother had this method too. She'd make pencil sketches and then use them for oil paintings. For ideas, you'd use parts of them. Parts of sketches are useful. Parts are of no use. But it's useful to have the notes on the animals and the colors. I never liked taking photographs. Somehow the camera doesn't see what your eye sees. I liked to get what my eye saw.

MBG: Do you have to be fond of an animal to paint it?

Ipcar: I don't know. Horses are very impressive and beautiful. I remember someone who was blind and then when they could see a horse, they were so disappointed. They thought it would be much more beautiful. They must have looked at the wrong kind of a horse.

SEVEN:

Emergencies, Crises & Tragedies

LARGE ANIMAL RESCUE

U p ahead on the interstate, there is a trailer overturned with two horses inside. The ambulance and firefighters have arrived and are taking the injured driver and passenger to the hospital.

You're a horse person and you want to help. You see the horses still stuck in the trailer. The trailer is on its roof, just yards from traffic. You introduce yourself to the firefighter in charge, tell him you're a horse person, jump in, and save the day, right? Wrong!

Many of us horse folk carry this attitudinal badge: I know horses therefore I can solve any horse-related problem. That might work around the coffee table. But when it comes to incidents like this one, it just isn't true. More often than not, the horse person ends up getting in the way and putting him- or herself in harm's way.

We let our emotion toward equines overtake all reason and protocol. Our good intentions can and do impede the rescue process. It's no surprise that so many human rescues are caused by ill-fated animal rescues.

Animal rescue expert, Dr. Tomas Gimenez, likes to tell the story of an entire fire department deployed to free a goose from a frozen lake. "It's not about the goose!" he says. Nor is it about the deer in traffic, or the cat in a tree, or a dog in a culvert, says Gimenez. It's about avoiding the potential chaos and tragedy that can ensue when amateurs attempt to rescue that animal. "Animal incidents are more emotional than human incidents," says Gimenez. "And that's when people get hurt."

On the flip side, successful animal rescue makes great press. You'd better believe a rescued horse will appear in the next day's paper. Rescuers (fire departments or animal welfare organizations, or otherwise) can count on a healthy uptick in donations and positive public relations as well. One department in England reported that three-fourths of their media coverage involved animal rescue, says Gimenez.

So, let's get back to the road rollover. How should you respond?

- Identify yourself as a competent horse handler.
- Offer to do whatever will help, even if it does not relate to the horses.
- Stay out of the way.

I became certified in Technical Large Animal Emergency Rescue through an intensive, three-and-a-half-day course led by Gimenez and his ex-wife, Dr. Rebecca Gimenez, of South Carolina and Georgia, respectively. They travel across the country and abroad, teaching this excellent course with morning lectures and presentations.

They have a well-stocked library of rescues done right and gone wrong. We viewed a wide range of footage—from tragic livestock trailer accidents involving dozens of horses to a single trail horse wedged between a downed tree and a riverbank. We viewed the silly horse that got his front half over the gate but couldn't complete the task. And we pondered at the horses that got up into the hayloft but couldn't get down. Afternoons and evenings were devoted to hands-on problem solving.

Tomas and Rebecca travel with their able assistants—large animals, of course. On this tour, they brought Karma, a lovely strawberry roan walking horse gelding; Torque, a rescued Appaloosa gelding, and Fabio, a white llama.

Firefighters, paramedics, veterinarians, and people like me (who work with horses for a living) participated in the course. It was a healthy mix. The emergency personnel knew all about incident protocol but very little about horse behavior. And we knew horses but were fairly clueless about how best to act in an emergency.

Tomas and Rebecca like to point out that there is one constant similarity in all large animal incidents: They are all different and unpredictable! Even with their calm, well-heeled demonstration animals, each mock incident proved challenging.

We used snow fencing to corral Karma, Torque, and Fabio (who, with Rebecca's encouragement, did their best to behave like wild, uncontainable beasts). This technique, using one person for every ten-foot section of plastic fencing, would be useful for cordoning off several large animals, either to keep them away from a structure or to move them toward containment without directly handling them.

We extricated Karma from a trench using an A-frame, metal pipe structure, and a pulleys-and-ropes system. We threaded thick webbing (old fire hoses made of canvas) under his belly and safely lifted him out.

During this exercise, we learned that horses tend to struggle during take-offs and landings, i.e., when their hooves just leave the ground and when they are set back down.

When Karma was fully suspended, he hung like a kitten carried by the scruff of its neck. He was limp and seemed relaxed. As soon as he touched ground, though, he had had quite enough of the webbing and ropes.

We extracted a horse stuck up to his chest in mud. It wasn't Karma or Torque. This time, we used a seven-hundred-pound equine mannequin.

Did you know that you can really, really hurt a horse if you just throw on a halter and try to yank him out of the mud? Stuck-in-the-mud incidents are all too common because of the incredibly small surface area for such a heavy animal. "You have one thousand two hundred pounds on four toothpicks," says Tomas. It is vital to eliminate the suction before trying to extract anything from mud. We accomplished this task by inserting metal tubes in and around our horse dummy. Each tube was rigged to a water supply. The tubes were perforated, allowing water to seep out every few inches. It flowed in and around the horse's legs. After feeding thick webbing around its torso, we were able to pull the mannequin out of the muck.

For our night search and rescue exercise, we tracked down Karma and his panicky, head-injured rider in the woods of New Gloucester, Maine. First, of course, we treated the rider. Then we dealt with recumbent Karma, meaning he could not stand. For this exercise, he was carefully sedated and monitored by two on-scene veterinarians.

We wrapped his mock broken leg and placed it in a secure splint. Then, we placed webbing in front of his hind legs and behind his front legs. We moved him onto a rescue glide (a large, thick piece of plastic which can be pulled by ropes or cables) and transported him to safer ground.

The theme throughout these incidents and, indeed, their entire coursework remained the same: If you can't rescue the horse safely, then you can't rescue the horse.

Tomas and Rebecca have participated in many successful rescues and improved the animal rescue operations of scores of departments. They also have nightmare stories of rescues gone horribly wrong, where horses and rescuers have perished. Their experiences, recounted with wisdom, candor, and humor, make the course all the more poignant.

There is a well-documented element of learning from mistakes in their teachings. Simple mistakes—like someone throwing a rope around a horse's neck and trying to pull it to safety or stepping into a crashed trailer to free a horse—are completely avoidable.

As Tomas told us about one hero who climbed into a trailer and freed a desperate horse, "Once freed, the horse is not going to stop and say, 'Excuse me. I would like to get out now. Would you please step aside?'"

At the end of the day, I asked myself how we, as horse owners and Good Samaritans, can help in the event of a disaster or emergency incident.

Here are some suggestions:

- Contact your county or state emergency management agency and ask how you can get involved in their animal rescue training, plans, and operations.
- Contact your local fire department, emergency response units, and animal shelters, and ask what they have for training and how you can get involved.
- Take an Incident Command System course, offered by FEMA at various locations and online.

VITAL TRAINING THROUGH TRAGEDY

Sometimes tragedy can provide vital training. This was the lesson behind my animated (some might say crass) call home from the Equine Affaire.

"Guess what?" I asked over the phone. "We moved a dead horse."

Sure, my intention was to shock my unflappable teenagers. I neglected to communicate the deep sympathy I felt for the poor owner and her horse. That would come later in the conversation.

But I get ahead of myself...

My friend, Michelle Melaragno, and I had the opportunity to put our training to use as we assisted in the evacuation of a euthanized horse. It wasn't fun, but we appreciated the chance to practice what we've been taught as large animal rescuers.

We just don't get chances to move thousand-pound recumbent animals. This is not like swaddling a dead cat in a towel. It's extremely challenging to move them quickly, safely, and humanely and we were honored to have this serendipitous practice.

We didn't get the whole story from the owner but surmised this much from several bystanders' observations at this major horse event in Springfield, Massachusetts:

The owner pulled into the Barn E grounds, hauling her twelve-year-old mare in a double trailer with ramp. When she went to back the horse out, the horse stumbled at the ramp's top corner, somehow flipped over backward, and "folded like a pretzel" said one witness.

The owner and those coming to help decided the injury was severe enough that the horse should stay down. They covered her with a blanket and called the Equine Affaire's on-call vet.

He arrived quickly and evaluated her. She'd fractured one of her hind legs above the hock. He recommended euthanasia.

This is when my friend Michelle and I arrived at Barn E. We had raced there upon hearing news of a horse down. We were eager to help in any way and we were hoping, of course, that the horse would be saved.

After learning of the mare's sad fate, we raced back to the Breed Pavilion where we had seen a large animal rescue display, sponsored by the Animal Rescue League of Boston.

We needed their Rescue Glide (a large, thick sheet of plastic with open slats for securing ropes) and their help. They generously and immediately provided both.

Back at Barn E, I spoke with the owner, the on-call vet, Brenda Martin, a helpful bystander and experienced horsewoman, and Dr. Chris D'Orazio, the medical director of the equine ambulance, stationed nearby at Barn C.

I made sure it was alright to help and to take pictures. I identified myself and Michelle as not affiliated with any organization but nonetheless qualified to help.

Michelle directed efforts to move the horse off the mud and onto the glide and then into the owner's trailer. We wrapped the mare's head in a towel and two women supported it by holding the corners of the towel. (A horse head and neck can weight about one hundred fifty pounds, so this was no small feat.)

It took a well-coordinated, six-person effort to move the horse into the trailer. Once there, Michelle wisely hobbled the legs while they were still flexible. Rigor mortis would set in during the owner's ride back to New Hampshire. Straight, rigid legs would make it very tough to get the dead horse out of the trailer.

It was a quick, respectful process completed in front of dozens of bystanders. In less than ten minutes, we moved the horse in a dignified manner. I would like to think we did the horse and owner a service. How horrible it would have been if the process was clumsy and drawn out.

I should add that most everyone involved had some large animal rescue training and we worked very well as a team. If the incident had been more involved, it would have been helpful to appoint an "incident commander," someone to direct our actions. But given the situation, we managed well with many Indians and no chief.

FIRST RESPONDER COURSE

Six days into my Wilderness First Responder course, after yet another ten hours of lectures and rescue simulations, I got a little giddy. Up to then, the course, offered by Wilderness Medical Associates at the Chewonki Foundation in Wiscasset, Maine, was a jumbled mass of acronyms and protocols. Sure, the instructors were fabulous and my classmates were inspiring. But I was quietly gagging on the sheer mass of information we needed to ingest.

- When do you really worry about a head injury?
- When do you stop CPR?
- You have two critical patients. Only one can be evacuated. Who do you choose and why?

We learned the Patient Assessment System on Day One. But it took six days to truly absorb it and put it to proper use. With or without the litany of abbreviations, I could finally approach a mock patient with confidence.

"Hi, my name is Maddy and I'm here to help you. Can you tell me what's wrong?"

I helped a patient with heat stroke. I helped another who'd fallen from a tree, gouged up his leg, and knocked his head. I helped one poor fellow with a dislocated shoulder. The pushy, drunken loudmouth? I helped him away from the scene so my fellow rescuers could help his friends.

For years, I've worked with horses and have developed my own wellness checklist. It's become an intuitive process. Usually, it's just me and a quiet, cooperative, four-legged patient. If it's bad, I call more knowledgeable friends or the vet.

But human patients? They talk back. They moan and scream. They question. They faint. They give me stress. Granted these were scenarios with made-up victims and simulated wounds, but before the course, I'm pretty sure I would have been a dubious rescuer. I might have panicked. I might have done harm.

My head instructor, Eric Duffy, would say I drank the WMA Kool Aid. But drinking Kool-Aid suggests you're buying into something without critical examination. It also suggests the drink might be bad for you.

I'd rather think of myself as another WMA fish. The bait? A course to give me skills and training for critical thinking when something bad happens in the woods. The hook? Confidence acquired by knowing I have these skills and training so I can help folks when something bad happens in the woods. Now I can help the horse AND the rider.

R.I.P., ANTHONY SHADID

When he died, it struck me as completely unfair. First, Anthony Shadid was a brilliant journalist in the prime of his career, covering one of the most important stories in the world. Second, horses were to blame.

Shadid, a two-time, Pulitzer-Prize-winning reporter for the *New York Times*, collapsed near the Turkey-Syria border after having an allergic reaction to horses.

I admired Shadid for years. He worked for the *Boston Globe* when I was a correspondent there. In 2002 he was shot while on assignment for the *Globe* in the West Bank. I remember when he was arrested, held, and physically abused by Libyan authorities.

To cover the civil war and state crackdown in Syria, Shadid sought help from smugglers and guides. They had crossed the border from Turkey by horseback and under cover of darkness. He had a moderate allergic reaction then but recovered after resting, according the Tyler Hicks, the *New York Times* photographer who had accompanied him.

On the return trip, the team took measures to stay away from the horses, but Shadid nonetheless reacted to the horse allergens on the smugglers' clothes. He struggled to breathe and collapsed. Hicks administered CPR but could not revive him. It was unclear if any medication was available or administered.

Of course, horses are not literally blamed. But horse allergens and the lack of intervention are what killed Shadid.

As horsemen and women, we deal with certain risks associated with handling big, powerful animals. But allergies? Asthma attacks triggered by our beloved equines?

According to an article in *Slate*, twenty million Americans have asthma; less than four thousand die from attacks annually. That's a tiny fraction considering asthma's prevalence. The death rate is fewer than one per one hundred thousand, less than those who die by accidental drowning.

With so many asthmatics and so few mortalities, it's clear that prevention and treatment have been effective. Most of the deaths occur because the individuals lacked ordinary medication or failed to take it correctly.

Dr. James Sublett, a fellow at the American College of Allergy, Asthma, and Immunology, told the *Washington Post* that about 10 percent of Americans are allergic to animals in general. Sublett said much more is known about dog and cat allergies; there's not a lot of research done on horses in this field.

I'm guessing most of you know if you're allergic to horses and deal with it. But what if you're with someone who's allergic? What to do? I'm not really allergic to anything, and this scenario tested my training as a Wilderness First Responder.

My friend, Tom O'Grady, did the right thing when he first saw his daughter react to horses. "We were apple picking with friends, and one of the options at the orchard was to go on a horse-drawn wagon ride. Just getting close to the horse put Siobhan into really bad shape—eyes red and puffy, difficulty breathing. I had to find a pharmacy quickly to buy some Benadryl. Scary."

Be aware that some folks can have sudden, severe reactions. Have Benadryl in your first aid kit or home medicine cabinet.

Tom's daughter, Siobhan O'Grady, shared her history, experiences, and treatments. "The symptoms I feel are completely asthmatic. Within a few minutes of being near anyone who is wearing clothes with horse hair on them, being in a house where horseback riders live, or being near a horse, my eyes get itchy and red, and my throats gets scratchy as well.

"I can usually maintain the reaction with Claritin during the day and Benadryl at night. If I were to actually ride a horse, I would get a strange rash of perfect dots all around my eyes, and my eyes would turn puffy. My throat closes up, my chest starts to feel trapped, and I can't get any kind of oxygen. My immediate instinct is to lie down on my back with my arms straight out, which opens up my airways.

"I also need to take my Albuterol inhaler immediately and a triple dose of Benadryl. My symptoms usually subside within an hour or two of me being away from a horsey environment. If I couldn't treat myself and was in a horse environment, then I honestly wouldn't be surprised if I had a similar fate to Anthony...I feel seriously desperate when I'm near a horse."

Dr. Cynthia Dechenes, of Topsham (Maine) Family Medicine, told me that most asthmatics are treated like Siobhan with inhalers (like Albuterol) for mild cases and oral steroids (like Prednisone) for more serious bouts.

In a wilderness setting like Shadid's, it would be important to have those medications available, as well as Benadryl and even an Epipen. (A treatment for anaphylactic shock, it is a medical device used to deliver a measured dose of epinephrine. Anaphylactic shock is a severe allergic reaction characterized by a sharp drop in blood pressure and difficulty breathing.)

Most of us can get to an emergency room within the hour. But what if you can't? Who knows if Shadid's death could have been prevented?

As Dechenes reminded me, war zones are full of tragic deaths from simple, seemingly preventable causes. "During wars, think of how many millions of people have died from infection...Think of the aid worker who dies in a bus accident," she said.

So I'm trying to take a lesson from this sad event: Be aware and be prepared.

HORSES & COMBAT STRESS

Combat stress and horse death don't often collide. But it appears that's what happened when Ryan Grafft, a thirty-two-year-old captain in the National Guard, allegedly shot three horses, killing one of them.

After admitting to the shooting, Grafft told the Johnson County officials it was a "stupid" thing to do, according to the criminal complaint. He's been charged with three counts of livestock abuse and two counts of reckless use of a firearm.

Grafft went to Iraq in September 2005. His tour was nearly finished when then-President George W. Bush announced plans to increase America's presence in Iraq. Grafft stayed there for nearly two years.

As an infantry platoon leader in the 133rd Infantry Battalion, he led forty soldiers on more than five hundred combat logistical patrols, escorting sixty-two thousand trucks in Anbar province, one of the most dangerous areas, according to the *Mitchell County Press News*. Two soldiers in his battalion were killed. Thirty-five were injured.

"We saw a lot of IEDs (Improvised Explosive Devices)," Grafft told the local paper. "It wasn't an easy time."

Now, five years later, Grafft allegedly shoots and kills an innocent, unwitting animal.

It's easy to call acts like these "random violence," so why is the American public increasingly weary of stories like these? Nowadays, they seem as predictable as the next eruption of an active volcano. The government says it's helping soldiers deal with post traumatic stress, but with the uptick in crimes like these, it makes one wonder.

I spoke with a Johnson County prosecutor about the case. She told me the charges were all misdemeanors. Even if convicted, it's unlikely he'll serve any time in prison, she said.

MY HORSE ALMOST DIED

It was Halloween night five years ago—my scariest night as a horse owner. My horses were staying across the street because we hadn't yet fenced off enough land to have them stay comfortably at home. My kind, eighty-five-year-old neighbor had invited me to keep them at her spacious barn and pasture. It was a great arrangement. They kept her little Shetland pony company. I took care of everything. She kept on eye on things when I wasn't there. Or so I thought.

The previous night, I had fed them and noticed Handsome, my thoroughbred, seemed a bit off. I climbed on him bareback, and we moved around the pasture. He was willing but not his lively self. I fed him. He was a bit off his feed but he ate it. I went home.

The next day was the same, but it didn't occur to me to call a vet. He was eating, standing, and his behavior didn't seem to wave a red flag. Yellow, but not red.

On Halloween night, however, it got terrible real quickly. I arrived at the farm after my son's trick-or-treating. It was dark. Handsome was stumbling around the pasture. He had busted through the small paddock area in which I kept them every night. He was acting like he didn't even see the fencing. The area had been turned into a war zone with downed fencing and electric wire strewn across an acre. Handsome was frantic and struggling to get his bearings.

When I approached him, he didn't recognize me. When I tried to put a hand on him, he reacted as if I had jolted him with a Taser. Once, when I was trying desperately to get a line on him, he jumped away from me into the fence. That startled him so he rebounded and jumped into me. I went down. He went down, then clamored up and stumbled away. All in the pitch dark.

I finally was able to contain him in his stall and get a halter on him. But even then, the situation was desperate. He pressed his head into the corner, using his head as a fifth leg to try to stay balanced and upright. When he swayed too much to one side, he would drag and scrape his head along the stall boards until he got to the next corner. He'd remain wedged there until he lost balance again, and then he'd scrape himself to the next corner. It was horrific to watch.

I called an emergency vet line. I had just returned to Maine and hadn't established myself with one particular vet yet. This vet told me she couldn't make it and mumbled some explanation. [I later learned this vet had a habit of not attending to emergencies when she didn't feel like it. Argh!]

I finally managed to reach Dr. Charlie Brown at Annabessacook Veterinary Clinic in Monmouth. I described the sudden, strange, and desperate turn of events. I think she didn't believed me. But in an hour, she was at the barn. What's more: She got into the stall and, incredibly, managed to draw blood and medicate Handsome.

Five hours and critical blood tests later, she returned. Charlie told me it looked like some sort of infection had mushroomed more or less overnight. (What was the source of the infection? We'll never know.)

She hooked up an IV unit from the ceiling of his stall and administered massive doses of DMSO and antibiotic. "We're either going to save him or kill him," she said with a weary smile.

We saved him. But it was a long haul back to health. Dr. Brown set me up with IV meds for the next ten days so I could avoid the additional costs of sending him to Annabessacook or having her make multiple farm calls.

If you know thoroughbreds, you also know they drop weight when they sneeze. It took months and a veritable buffet of delicacies to get back the weight that Handsome lost during this crisis.

I learned some valuable lessons: If you board or are away from home a lot, make sure someone is accountable for assessing your horses. Only after the fact did my elderly neighbor tell me Handsome had been lying down an awful lot in the previous few days.

If you suspect a problem, make note of it and double your efforts to determine its cause and take preventive measures. Start keeping notes. Make sure your vet will come when you call. Think ahead. Decide how much you can afford. Share your limitations immediately with the vet before you get in over your head.

HORSE TRAUMA SAFETY NET – GOT YOURS?

It's been six years since I had to make an emergency vet call. In hindsight, I suppose we were due.

My horse, Brooke, hurt both front legs in an early morning fluke accident. The wounds were at and below her knees and sizeable. One was a V-shaped gash of three inches or so. The other was smaller but deeper. At first, I thought I could manage the care on my own. I cleaned them with Betadine and warm water, bandaged them, and wrapped the legs with gauze and Vetrap.

Brooke is a smart, pragmatic girl. She seemed to know I was trying to help and she let me tend to her with little fuss. But I was worried. I took a lot of pictures, sent them to two friends more knowledgeable than me, Michelle Melaragno and Dr. Rebecca Gimenez, instructors in large animal emergency rescue. They both responded, "Get the vet!"

I called Dr. Jeff Fay at Annabessacook. He arrived soon thereafter. Fay commended me for the initial care but said that if these lacerations had been left to heal on their own, the recovery would have been much longer and less certain.

He sedated her with Dormosedan, then applied and injected Lidocaine, a local anesthetic. With Brooke now blissfully oblivious, Fay was able to clip away hair, scrub the wounds, and lift the large, triangular flap of flesh to clean thoroughly underneath it. He dosed her again with Dormosedan and Lidocaine when she took issue with his actions. I could never have cleaned the wounds as well, especially without sedation!

Next, Fay stapled the triangular flap back in place. He pulled some flesh together with hand sutures and left a small opening at the bottom for possible drainage. I counted twenty staples and five sutures. Upon examining the other smaller, deeper cut, he noted partial ligament damage. He closed that wound with about eight staples.

We agreed that since she was walking so well, x-rays weren't necessary at this point. If the healing failed to progress at an expected rate, or, if there was excessive swelling and drainage, he said, we might suspect bone bruising or other damage.

"Let's wait and see," he told me. I was immensely pleased with his efficiency and expertise.

We bandaged her with Telfa pads, cotton, and Vetrap and left her to her hay. Later I checked the bandages and put a blanket on the poor girl. She was shivering as the sedation wore off, a common reaction.

Three days later, Brooke was doing well. She stood calmly for bandage changes. She was a wonderful patient and seemed to know how to take care of herself. She moved slowly and carefully around the enclosure. She was still the alpha mare, but she managed it with less physicality. Head turns and lip curls kept the others in line.

We faced a long recovery with diligent hygiene and doses of bute and antibiotic. There may be bumps in the road, but I'm sure I took the right turn when I called for help, despite the pain in my checkbook.

It brought to mind some issues we all should tackle before the crisis arrives: Do you have a first aid kit? Do you have a safety net? Optimally, this safety net includes the first aid kit, a reasonable knowledge of wound care, a predetermined budget for emergency care, (This visit costs $475. My last emergency call in 2005 cost $1,700. Ouch!), contact numbers of friends and emergency vet at the ready. It wasn't fun. But I'm thankful for horse friends to give their opinion and offer help, a kind and able vet at the ready, the chance to learn and improve my horse care, for the injuries not being worse.

EMERGENCY NECESSITIES

It helps if the horse is haltered. That's what I was thinking when driving along Maine Route 24 in Bowdoinham one day. There, dashing across the road, were two big Belgians. Partners in crime, you could say. They trotted through one yard and began helping themselves to the neighbors' lovely green pasture, er, lawn. No halters. No owner.

A sheriff's deputy happened on the scene, but he sheepishly admitted to 'not being a horse person.' (He might've been more of a horse person if there was less horse, I think.)

The neighbor grabbed a bag of carrots from her fridge. I grabbed the dog leash from my car, took off my belt to serve as another lead line, and together we got them back into their barn without too much fuss.

But the incident got me thinking about a Whatcha-Gotta-Have Kit. Beyond the no-brainers, what other things should I have? What should every horse owner have?

No-brainers: I have some really simple things I carry on me all the time. It's not emergency stuff, but I'm always surprised by how often I use these few items—a belt, a knife, and a cell phone.

The belt doubles as a leash or lead line. The knife comes in handy for cutting bailing twine, peeling fruit, cutting the t-shirt so you can apply a tourniquet after you've cut yourself with the knife. (The other worst case scenario I envision is getting my foot caught in the stirrup, being dragged by the panicky horse, then valiantly cutting myself free with the knife.) The cell phone is for timing your heart rate, er, your horse's heart rate, and calling for help.

But, enough of those everyday, gotta-have items. Now for the emergency kit:

- Emergency contact info: phone numbers for your vet, your back-up vet, neighbor, horse-knowledgeable friend, someone with a trailer if you don't have one.
- A watch or someway to tell time and measure seconds and minutes (cell phone)
- A few bundles of Vetrap

- Banamine paste
- Gas X (that's the brand name for a human OTC medicine for indigestion)
- Assorted syringes
- Stretch bandages
- 4x4 gauze pads
- Chlorhexadine scrub for cleaning wounds (a common name brand for this is Nolvasan.)
- Instant cold pak for you and/or your horse
- Thermometer
- Stethoscope
- Vetropolycin ointment for eye or around-eye injury
- Saline solution – for washing out eye injury or irritant
- Antibiotic ointment
- Hoof pic
- Catheter to rinse out a puncture wound (Make sure you have a syringe that fits it.)
- First Aid tape for bandaging
- Duct tape
- Kotex/small diapers – good, relatively cheap first aid pads
- Polo wraps – for covering bandages
- Hoof-shaped poultice pads – pricey but more convenient and less messy than poultice
- Latex gloves
- Leatherman, or similar multi-tool.
- Halter (preferably a rope halter with lead line attached. Rope halters readily fit more sizes of horses than other halters.)
- Treats

As I was reviewing this list, I realized there is also knowledge every horse owner needs:

- How to recognize signs and symptoms of colic and how to treat it
- How to clean and dress various wounds
- How to treat other injuries (like strains)
- How to take horse's temperature, respirations and heart rate
- How to recognize signs and symptoms of heat distress and how to treat it

FIELD CRISIS
By Lauren Fraser

Lauren Fraser runs Good Horsemanship from her home in British Columbia, Canada. I met her a few years ago at the Mane Event in Red Deer, Alberta. Since then, we've kept in touch, and I recently learned of this crisis with one of Lauren's geldings. For a few Canadian phrases, the American equivalent is in parentheses.

My husband Dave and I live at the foot of the coastal mountains in Squamish, British Columbia, Canada. We have a ritual morning walk around our property, which we claim is for the benefit of our eldest dog's health, but we both enjoy it too.

Part of the pleasure is seeing my herd of eight horses grazing the twenty-five acres. Fall had recently come to the valley, and the horses responded to the cooler weather by putting on a great display of running, bucking, and farting their way around the property. We watched for around five minutes, and as they began to wind down, Dave started wandering back towards the house.

That's when I noticed the fresh trail of bright red blood droplets, spaced very close together, on the ground. I shouted to Dave and ran to the front field where the horses had galloped. I could see the herd circling around, starting to slow, although they were still prepared to run at the slightest sudden movement. I forced myself to walk calmly towards them, visually searching through the bodies and legs for any sign of blood.

Standing slightly off from the other five horses, my "bachelors"—three bonded geldings—stood, breathing hard, muscles tense. One of those bachelors was my new four year old colt, Calcite. I saw with horror the bright red blood pumping from his groin and down his left hind leg with each heartbeat.

I worked for many years as a veterinary assistant in both small animal and mixed practice hospitals, and also have professional training as an occupational first aid attendant. I knew that without immediate pressure to stop the bleeding, Calcite was going to die before me. I've assisted in similar horse calls with my veterinarian husband over the years, and I pride myself on my abilities in an emergency situation.

Usually having this knowledge is a blessing, but today it was a curse. Understanding that Cal was bleeding out before my eyes, I temporarily "lost my sh&t", and I panicked.

I had a hay string (baling twine) in my pocket, and I grabbed for Cal to catch him, which, understandably, pushed him to run away from me. The blood pumped faster, and a large pool formed when he stopped twenty feet away from me. To force myself to calm down, I approached one of his bachelor buddies, and gave him a scratch instead. Then I sidled my way towards Cal. I managed to slip the hay string around his neck, and attempted to stop the flow of blood, which came from high up in his groin, with pressure from my hand. No luck.

Cal was panicky and wheeled around, causing me to almost lose my grip on the string. My husband shouted for me to get him closer to the house, and he ran to get sedative from the medical kit. I started leading Cal up, thinking only of negative outcomes for the situation we found ourselves in. Just a few months prior, I had unexpectedly lost my Horse Number One and I was still raw over his loss; the thought of tragically losing another horse weighed heavy.

Part II: Trying to Stop the Flow and Getting Help
Luckily, the horses had stopped near the gate to the arena, so it was a relatively short walk for Cal. Once there, I haltered him and attempted to apply pressure to the wound with my toque (wool hat).

I had acquired Cal six months prior, as a three-year old from Idaho. Although he was raised right, he was still wild in many ways when I got him. I had spent a great deal of time taming Cal, but in his panicked state, with me slowly shoving a toque up into his groin to stop the flow, it was not something he wanted to be part of. His panic just made him bleed faster.

I dropped the toque and managed instead to find the vessel with my fingers, and applied pressure, which slowed the bleeding. My husband appeared, and gave Cal an intravenous sedative, taking into account his blood loss so far. He also took over the pressure while I held Cal's rope.

My mother's house faces the arena. From her vantage she spied the two of us, and the palomino horse covered in blood. She came out, offering help, and Dave sent her back inside for the phone and some towels.

We live three hours from an equine hospital, and although we have a small medical kit, we didn't have the additional drugs to safely drop Cal, nor the surgery kit to close the wound.

While Dave waited for the phone, he probed the laceration with his fingers and found a finger-sized stick inside. He pulled it out, examined the wound, and discovered Cal had lacerated a large femoral vein. Dave crouched next to the sedated Cal and continued applying pressure.

After reaching my equine vet, Dave came up with a drug cocktail we could acquire from the local small animal vet to drop Cal and suture the wound. It wasn't the best combination of drugs—Cal's recovery could be rough. If he thrashed around the chances of opening the wound again were high. But at that point it, was our only option.

A call was made to our neighbor, an AHT (vet tech) at the local small animal clinic, and she agreed to drive us out the supplies. Dave had managed to find the magic combination of pressure and location that was controlling the bleeding, so all we could was wait the thirty minutes for our neighbor to arrive.

The slowest minutes in the history of horse ownership had passed after the phone call to the clinic, when something startled Cal, and he suddenly lurched forward. Dave lost his hold on the blood vessel. But before he could reapply it, we noticed that the bleeding had stopped.

There was still some oozing, but not the pumping we had seen before. A clot had formed in the vein. Would it hold? We all stood very, very still, hoping that nothing would cause Cal to shy again.

Our neighbor showed up shortly after, with the supplies we would need to drop Cal and suture the vessel. But Dave was reluctant to perform the surgery if we could get by without it.

Dropping Cal had its own complications, and if we could keep him quiet, we might be able to avoid it.

So we waited. And waited. And waited. OK, I was paranoid, and ended up keeping him immobile for five hours before I was convinced the clot would hold. Late in the afternoon I walked him the short trip to a small paddock for the night, with a neighbor horse for company to keep him calm.

I didn't sleep well that night, even after a few post-accident fingers of single malt whiskey. Visions of the clot not holding, and Cal bleeding out while I slept had me up throughout the night. By morning I was convinced that it was safe to haul him to my vet three hours away for a recheck to make sure all of the stick was out.

I loaded up my mare for company, and put the wobbly and weak Cal in behind her. I'll admit it, that trip was the only time I've ever coveted those in-trailer video cameras, but truth be told, had he started bleeding again there would be little I could do by myself on the side of the highway.

I got to the clinic and unloaded. My vet took blood before we sedated him, to find out if his blood loss was significant enough to require a transfusion. His packed cell volume (a measure of his red blood cells) was low enough that he did, but he was eating and drinking well, and I had brought a mare along instead of a gelding. (Horses of the same gender are better donors.)

My vet sedated Cal and got the ultrasound probe on the wound. They couldn't visualize the end of the puncture, as it ran deep between the fascia and his muscle, well beyond the distance the ultrasound could image. From what they could see they were fairly sure that no stick remained. They flushed the wound, gave him a tetanus injection, and sent us home on antibiotics.

Cal was weak for about ten days post-accident, but the wound healed well, and he was soon back to normal. Although I've worked within the veterinary field for most of my life, being "the client" briefly caused me to forget my skills and training in the middle of a life-and-death emergency involving one of my own. Although I've worked within the veterinary field for most of my life, being "the client" briefly caused me to forget all of my skills and training in the middle of a life-and-death emergency that involved one of my own.

If I could share the reminders I apparently needed to review with fellow horse owners before the next potential horse emergency, they would be this:

1. Stop. Breathe. Assess the situation. Proceed calmly. Horses pick up on our emotional state. A frightened prey animal doesn't respond well to a frightened predator trying to grab him.

2. Take a horse-specific first aid course, and build a first aid kit. Although Cal's laceration was in an area we couldn't apply a pressure bandage, we did have on hand diapers and bandages for such situations. A horse first aid kit doesn't need to be costly, and could save your horse's life.

3. Having a hay string in your pocket at all times isn't such a bad thing.

4. Horses from Idaho don't take well to having toques shoved into their groins.

HORSES & NATURAL DISASTERS

The fire chief of tiny Chincoteague, Virginia (population 4,347), may not be a horseman, but he had an idea that the Chincoteague ponies would take care of themselves if given the chance. The manager of the Chincoteague National Wildlife Refuge thought so too.

Instead of containing them during Hurricane Sandy, the two departments, which together share responsibility and ownership of the herds, let them have the run of the place. "They had free range of the entire refuge," said manager Lou Hinds.

The hurricane did a ton of damage to Assateague and Chincoteague Islands, the thin slivers of sand that are as vulnerable as the Outer Banks when it comes to big storms. But the horses appeared to have weathered it just fine.

"Sometimes it's better," said Chief Harry Thornton, "To turn 'em out and let them 'em do what they know to do best. They knew something was up. We opened those gates. They knew it was time to head to higher ground." He said the ponies usually head to an area known as White Hills on Assateague Island, a sandy knoll that surrounds the historic lighthouse and rises twenty to twenty-five feet above sea level, according to the *Washington Post*.

HORSES IN TORNADOS – OH, MY!

What's a horse owner to do with this recent rash of tornado watches and warnings? It's certainly unusual for us Mainers.

I talked with a delightfully dry-humored spokesman for the National Weather Service in Gray, Maine. He said, "When it comes to livestock, you have to play the odds."

On one hand, you might not want to put them in a barn that's going to go down. On the other, you might not want them exposed to flying debris—like the roof of the barn that just blew down. And on the third hand, bringing them into the basement with you is probably not feasible. (I kid you not, he told me this without so much as a chuckle.)

BUT, he said, most tornadoes around here are weak, topping out with wind speeds of 80 to 100 miles per hour. AND, most barns around here are sound, post-and-beam construction. They can withstand a lot. Consider your barn, your surroundings, and the comfort levels of you and your equines. Or, just flip a coin.

A HORSE'S NO-WIN SITUATION

That was the tough, take-away message from Dr. Rebecca Gimenez when asked about how to protect your horses in the event of a tornado.

Close them in barns and you run the risk of harming them when the barn collapses. You may also stress them severely by taking away their ability to move and use their flight instinct. Leave them in the pasture; they may get hurt too.

Folks in tornado-prone states may be tempted to build fortified structures, she said, but these will cost a lot and compromise light and ventilation. (Think concrete bunkers)

Preventive measures are vital:

- Consider micro-chipping your horse.
- Braid contact information into their mane and/or paint it on your horse.
- Store or get rid of equipment or other things that may become airborne and harm your horse when it goes flying. (Think lawnmowers or that old bed frame around back)
- Take care of yourself, first and foremost. (If something happens to you, you won't be there for your horses.)

VET REFLECTS ON TORNADO

More than a month after an EF-5 tornado ripped apart Moore, Oklahoma, Dr. Clayton McCook paused to reflect on the damage, the recovery, and the prospects. EF-5 is a Level 5 tornado on the Enhanced Fujita scale; it is the highest level, with 'incredible' damage and winds over two hundred miles per hour.

McCook, an Oklahoma resident and Texas native, told me that from his observations and experience, nothing above ground can survive an EF-5. "The only people who survived were underground," he said.

His acquaintance saw twelve horses pulled up into the sky, like so many plastic grocery bags. "He told me the cloud sucked them up into the air," said McCook. Short of building an underground equine bunker or evacuating instantaneously, McCook said there's not a lot one can do, aside from attaching contact information to them (microchipping, paint, safety halter).

Some horses got lucky as the tornado skirted their pastures. Dozens were hospitalized or placed in foster care. As many Moore horse owners had their homes reduced to concrete slabs, they may never be in a position to take them.

McCook and Dan Mullenix have developed the non-profit Oklahoma Livestock First Responder team. When the Moore tornado hit, OLFR rescued, treated, and transported scores of horses from devastated grounds to places like Heritage Park, a local racetrack, which opened its doors to newly homeless equines.

As recovery efforts proceeded, some horses felt the impact of a new stress—confinement. It can be hard on any horse to be in a stall, but those that are used to paddocks and fields struggle more. Blue, a mare injured in tornado, recovered but was starting to weave in her stall. "I told them, 'We've got to get her out of here. These horses need to move out of stalls.'"

EIGHT:

Evidence-based Horsemanship (EBH)

WHAT IS EBH?

*E*vidence-Based Horsemanship is the book and umbrella term developed by Dr. Steve Peters and Martin Black. I helped the pair with the book's manuscript. And as Steve's significant other, I traveled and reported on EBH-related engagements. I've had time and opportunity to digest and reflect on this far-reaching model.

The term, 'evidence-based,' has been tossed around in the medical field for years. In health insurer terms, it pretty much means 'if you can't show that it works, we're not paying for it.'

Insurance companies demand that hospitals and physicians back up their costs with research to show that what they're charging for has been proven effective, i.e., worth reimbursement. In other words, Insurance Company A is not going to pay for Treatment B just because Doctor C has always prescribed it. Research (clinical studies, physicians' observations, patient feedback, etc.) needs to support it.

Working within the evidence-based framework is how insurance companies help manage costs and steer folks away from unproven or ineffective treatments.

So what is Evidence-Based Horsemanship (EBH)?

Peters and Martin Black propose we adopt the same attitude when it comes to horse training and management. Just because you've always done it or someone important tells you so, doesn't mean it's the best thing for you and your horse.

Only when research supports it does the horsemanship become preferable and favored. Research, in this case, is Peters's scientific findings on horse brain function and Martin Black's observations of thousands of colts and adult horses.

I saw EBH at work when I visited Peters and Black at a clinic in Lisbon Falls, Maine. As the morning session got under way, one rider struggled with her worried, agitated young horse. Black told her to let him graze.

What? Isn't this a no-no?

Peters explained how grazing helps engage the parasympathetic nervous system, the relaxation-oriented part of the autonomic nervous system. If the rider had yanked on the reins and tried to contain the horse, she might have evoked a response from the sympathetic nervous system. That's when animals are likely to react with a fight-or-flight response, i.e., bucking, bolting, etc.

Sure enough, a few minutes of grazing helped put the horse in a better frame of mind. He was more ready to learn.

What Evidence-Based Horsemanship Isn't
One of the nice things about EBH is the lack of ulterior motive. There is no line of EBH halters and lead lines. There is no magic stick.

As Peters writes:

> "EBH is an approach that continually evolves as our knowledge base grows. Finding that one has done something the wrong way may be just as valuable as getting it right if it refines the knowledge base so others do not have to struggle with a similar wrong turn. This approach is not concerned with arguing over a school of thought or following one trainer over another. Egos, persuasive salespeople, and charismatic personalities would have little relevance to EBH.
>
> "There is room for everyone under this umbrella to educate themselves by asking what does our current scientific knowledge of the horse, when applied and

empirically observed, show me about getting the best outcomes possible for me and the horse? Does it work? What's the proof? What is it based on?"

It is crucial to consider the evolution and development of wild horses when we look at the most effective methods for training and maintaining our domestic horses.

In their presentation, Black and Peters referenced the mustangs of the western United States as examples of horses in their natural, evolved state.

It's ideal, they say, to maintain domestic horses as close to that environment as possible. When you start messing with their environment, their upbringing, their food, and their movement, you invite problems.

"Understand where they came from," said Black as they showed a slide presentation of mustangs running on the Oregon range. "What did we do to screw them up? Try to get them back to there, their natural environment."

Horses have been around for fifty-five million years. The first horses were doglike, stood less than twenty inches high, and had three toes. The modern-day horse as we know it, Equus, is about four million years old and has one toe or hoof. Equus includes zebras, the asses and donkeys of Africa and Asia, and horses.

We started domesticating horses just four thousand years ago.

The following are examples of what happens when we deviate from the natural state:

Head restriction
Horse eyes are packed with cells along a lateral streak, giving them excellent vision straight ahead. They're good at seeing the horizon and approaching predators. They don't see well directly above or below. They need to move their heads to focus well in these ranges.

When riders limit their head movement by holding the reins tight or using restrictive tack, they take away the horses' need to look at the ground, look at the jump, look at an object.

Restriction can spell disaster. Peters and Black cited steeplechase as a sport, which could benefit from less rein contact and head restriction. "The horse is saying, 'Give me my head so I can see.' The horse still needs to see the ground to know when to leave the ground," said Black. "If you give the rider that responsibility, it's not reliable."

Stalls

Keeping a horse in a stall can create all kinds of problems from behavioral and nutritional to physical. Horses can't move or graze or interact healthily. They may compensate by picking up habits like weaving or cribbing. They may be susceptible to issues like laminitis and underdeveloped muscles. They may lack the crucial social and athletic skills otherwise acquired in a field with a herd.

Grain

Horses' digestive tracts are built for constant grazing. Most horses thrive on plain ol' grass along with plenty of exercise. Introducing grain can create issues similar to those of stall-bound horses.

Peters considered the prevalence of winter colic. Horses getting a lot of grain and little exercise, spell out a recipe for disaster along the digestive tract.

"Whisker" trimming

Those whiskers are actually vibrissae, hairs that serve as tactile organs. Trim them and you are depriving a horse of crucial sensory tool. When a horse comes close to an object (another horse, a tarp on the ground, etc.), it might look like it is sniffing it. But really, it is assessing it with its vibrissae, "to see if it's wet, dry, light, heavy, hot, cold," said Black. "Shaving them is like cutting off someone's fingers."

Futurities

Horses all over the world are prepared for futurities. Theoretically, futurities give the horse a chance to show off how great he will be down the line. It's a breeder's means for reaping an early reward. But horses in the wild don't prove themselves at age two. Black and Peters told us that horses are still developing neurologically, muscularly, and socially.

"You can have a brilliant first-grader become an idiot high-schooler," said Black, who prefers to wait several years before starting colts.

HORSE NEUROLOGY & HORSEMANSHIP

B lack and Peters have trail-blazed by connecting horse neurology with horsemanship. They know horses lack our frontal lobe— the part of the brain responsible for forming generalizations, plans, and strategies. Black and Peters don't have much taste for anthropomorphism, the attribution of human capacities to equine behavior:

"My horse gave me some payback when he decided to toss me."

OR

"He bucked me off, but then came back and said he was sorry."

Nonetheless, they still find it helpful to explain horse development and behavior, using people metaphors. You will hear them say things like: "Colts are like third-graders and need recess." OR "Let him go home and think on it."

That's because despite our mammoth differences, we share some similarities in the very basic development and composition of our nervous systems. We both have autonomic nervous systems (ANS), the largely involuntary regulators of our organs, muscles, glands, etc. The parasympathetic and sympathetic nervous systems are the chief elements of ANS.

The sympathetic nervous system is what we see in fight-or-flight situations. Let me suggest two scenarios:

Outing A

You're out for a pleasant ride on a nice, sunny day. Suddenly, an angry bear appears on your path. The sympathetic nervous system is called into action (of both you and your horse). It uses energy. Your blood pressure increases, your heart beats faster, and digestion slows down. Y'all beat feet!

When a horse has a sympathetic nervous system response, we see the whites of his eyes, his tense muscles, his flared nostrils. You know the look. In a horse brain dissection, as Peters pointed out, the trigeminal nerve runs over the eye, down the face to the jaw. That's why you will see the cluster of signs (white eyes, tight jaw, and lips) noted above.

Outing B

You're out for a pleasant ride on a nice, sunny day. This time, however, you decide to relax, hobble your horse, and chill for a bit. You and your horse hang out in a meadow. He grazes while you read and ponder life. Enter the parasympathetic nervous system. Your blood pressure decreases, your heart beats slower, and digestion can start. The parasympathetic nervous system is called upon in 'rest and digest' situations. When a horse has a parasympathetic response, he may lick his lips, blink, and cock one of his legs.

When we look at these two trail-riding episodes, we can also examine our differences. Here is where the horse's lack of frontal lobe might actually put him in a better spot. You, the rider, come away from the angry bear experience with nightmares and baggage. Every time you return to that spot, see a picture of a bear, talk about bear encounters, you freak.

In studies of Post Traumatic Stress Disorder (PTSD) patients, said Peters, chemical etchings on the brain can have the effect of turning traumatic experiences into super memories.

But if the horse has enough good experiences afterward, he will likely override that traumatic episode. Such is life without a frontal lobe. Or, as Black noted with classic Yogi Berra delivery, "If the world becomes good, the world becomes good."

After Outing B, the rider comes away from the experience by perhaps attaching the meadow, the smells, and the book all into one fond, romantic recollection. Rose-colored glasses are frontal lobe stuff, too. The horse, on the other hand, may recall that he got to eat at that meadow.

LIGHT BULB MOMENTS

A horse's learning is largely about positive feedback. From a brain chemistry standpoint, positive feedback is linked to the release of a chemical or neurotransmitter called dopamine. In barnyard terms, we can think of dopamine release as closely tied to the relief of pressure. In other words, horses want comfort and relief from pressure. They will seek out the dopamine release because, quite simply, it feels good to them.

If you're sensitive, observant, patient, and able, you can take advantage of that specific proclivity. You can make your riding cues more and more subtle. You can create a refined learning machine in your horse. At that point, your horse will perform incredible moves while you sit in the saddle, making near-invisible adjustments. And the crowd will roar.

But first, it's crucial to understand the horse's learning process.

Let's take the much beloved task of trailer loading as an example. The horse may load into a trailer and find a release of pressure as the trailer is closed up and he finds hay to eat. There may be a dopamine release and a learning moment here. Alternatively, the horse may pull back, get away from its owner, find relief of pressure, and get a dopamine release. The 'learning moment' might be even more reinforcing if he gets to graze. In other words, horses don't discriminate between these good and bad learning moments. They will search for the dopamine release regardless of how humans interpret their actions.

Another aspect of learning related to dopamine release is a horse's comfort level. A horse won't learn much if he's scared or really uncomfortable. Nor will the lesson hit home if he's bored or over-drilled. It's when you find a balance between these two ends of comfort that the best learning occurs.

Martin Black writes, "...when we get the balance just right, the horse can operate at a place where he is interested but not worried. The more he experiences operating in this place, the more he looks for this place because it feels good to him."

SOME NOTES ON NEUROLOGY

Ever watch a newborn stretch and make herky-jerky movements? You're watching the beginning stages of its neural and muscular development. With slides and anecdotes to support the science, Peters described how myelination (the crucial depositing of white fatty matter around nerve fibers) of a young horse directs its ability to move, learn, and mature.

Ever wonder why young horses do best with short spurts of training? Their neurological development is not unlike that of a grade school student. It is not yet developed enough to handle long periods of study.

Ever marvel at a horse's ability to perform intricate movements? It's not so much 'thinking' as it is relying on muscle memory, stored in the cerebellum.

The cerebellum, the tangerine-sized 'little brain,' is responsible for what we might call motor memory. We have a cerebellum, too: riding a bike or running a barrel pattern, those motor patterns are stored in the same area for both horses and humans.

Movement responses to cues (from a rider or from the environment) are likewise stored in the cerebellum. A horse can make a lightning-flash skip to avoid tripping into a gopher hole or switch leads on command, thanks to this structure.

❧ — ❧

You can help create a super-learning horse when you let the horse search for that reward itself rather than forcing it. Consider a creek crossing. As humans, we look for the 'correct response' of getting from one side to the other. But if we have to spur the horse into crossing, we're missing the point. "The more they can do on their own," said Black, "the better the horse."

When he was a boy, Black recalled, he saw a big difference between handling cattle when they were relaxed or scared. "It was almost like flipping a switch," he said. "I always had thought there was something chemical going on," said Black. "When Steve started explaining it all, it made perfect sense."

The key, said the pair, was to recognize the external physical manifestations of these internal chemical changes and to work at optimizing positive outcomes.

For instance, the horse seeks comfort. On a neurochemical level, one might say it seeks a state of equilibrium or homeostasis. By arousing it through training, we can move it away from that equilibrium. When we offer horses a place of comfort, they will find it and relish their return to equilibrium. In other words, you have to make a horse uncomfortable for him to appreciate comfort. "If you take him there and then come back, that's when he gets the drugs he likes," said Black. "The real art of horsemanship is how far to take him into that [state of discomfort]."

With knowledge gained from brain chemistry, learning, and memory, we can travel more smoothly and with fewer wrecks along our horsemanship journeys.

Peters isn't suggesting we do anything different than Tom Dorrance might have done. "Tom Dorrance probably would have been the best behavioral neurologist," he said.

NINE:
Research & Reviews

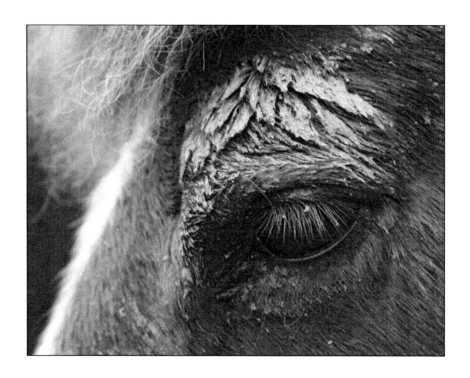

BEST HORSE PRACTICES

I founded the website, *BestHorsePractices*, in 2013. Its mission is to review equine research in laymen's terms, with an eye toward our everyday interactions with horses, and to give objective, science-based reviews of horse-related goods and services.

Ultimately, the best practices are those that are best for the health, welfare, and future of the horse. Not the human. *BestHorsePractices* advocates for those who feel the same. Together, we can improve horses' lives.

BETTER CARE – OUTSIDE THE BOX

Thanks, but I'd rather do without. My doctor looked at me sideways. Just because I'm down, doesn't mean I need an anti-depressant, I said. Time heals, I told him. And it did. I feel better.

Better care does not always mean using every medication, every treatment, or every technology at our disposal.

Unpasteurized cider won't kill us. Kids with attention deficit don't necessarily need to be drugged. That horse doesn't need asthma meds; he just needs get out of his stall and get some fresh air.

"Benign neglect is best." That's what Dr. Cynthia Reynolds told me when we were discussing horse care. "In the East, horses are loved to death," chimed in Elijah Moore, Reynolds's husband.

Once, there was no Smartpak. Once, there was no anti-bacterial anything. Once, there was no UnderArmor and five other layering options for horses.

When did we lose our faith in our horses' self-reliance and self-preservation? Why do we need to contract out their health and welfare to every commercial entity available? Where can I buy a bottle of intuition?

We spend billions on products to help our horses gain weight, lose weight, have shiny coats, run faster, run longer, recover better, etc. In our quest to optimize our horse's quality of life and performance, we can get lost in the miasma of choices made available to us. And so we listen and, to the delight of the horse product industry, we buy.

As consumers, we seem to have come to the conclusion that doing something, applying something, treating something, adding something, feeding something, blanketing something is somehow better than doing nothing.

This optimization pull is especially strong in the East. I chatted with a Triple Crown sales representative. He laughed at the contrast between the East and out West. "I was talking with a California woman who turns her horses out to a big pasture. She visits them once a week and wondered about grain," he said. "I'm sorry, ma'am, we don't have a Thursday feed."

"Martin always says that if you treat a horse like he's made of glass, then he'll break," said Kim Stone, a Maine horsewoman who's worked with Martin Black at the Alvord Ranch in Oregon. "He'd rather teach a horse to have some self-preservation."

I ran a not-so-scientific experiment the other week: My horse happened to cut herself just above her nose. It wasn't anything serious. Took the skin off a small area the size of a nickel.

A client's horse had a similar booboo. I made sure the area was clean and left it alone. My client scrubbed it with Nolvasan, then applied SWAT. Over several days, he repeated this procedure.

In a week, my horse's cut had scabbed over, sloughed off the scab, and completely healed. My client's horse's cut was still healing...slowly.

THE NOTION OF NATURE IS BEST

We know this much:

- Horses are designed to move a lot.
- Horses are meant to be with herd mates.
- Horses should have access to near-constant grazing but should get no grain.
- Horses should not be confined.
- Grooming, clipping, or shaving according to our perception of beauty and hygiene may interfere with the horse's ability to take care of themselves.
- Wild horses don't have the problems domestic horses have; overzealous care may actually compromise horses' well being instead of improving it.

This notion of Nature is Best model works brilliantly in the western United States where twenty acres often come with your house. But in many parts of the world, two acres is more like it.

If that's the case with you and your horses, Nature is Best takes effort. But with thought and diligence, you CAN follow the model. Your horses will probably thank you. It will be cheaper for you and likely less stressful for them.

Here are some possible modifications that embrace Nature is Best:

- Shelter: Offer cover for your horses but take down stall walls and metal bars that may separate them.
- Footing: Place pea stone or other hoof-friendly stone in high traffic areas. The gravel will help keep their hooves healthy and dry.
- Food: Wean them off grain. If you're concerned about the nutrition provided by your hay, have your hay tested. You can also look for deficiencies through blood work on individual horses. For horses needing to add more weight, consider soaked beet pulp, hay stretcher, and/or forage.
- Body regulation: Let your horses tell you they're cold, not the other way around. They will shiver to keep warm and become more anxious about food.
- Turnout: Give them room to move. If you have plenty of pasture, consider rotating them to optimize the grazing. If you have limited pasture, rotating them and supplementing with hay will work. If you have horses that don't get a lot of exercise and you worry about too much grazing, consider a dry, dirt paddock to keep them off grass for some periods of the day.
- Supplements: Studies show horses need next-to-no supplements with the possible exception of Vitamin E and selenium in regions where the grass and hay are deficient in those nutrients.

Blackfish (Nature is Best – Sidebar)

Blackfish is a movie about killer whales and how captivity makes them miserable and crazy. It's an easy concept for us horse owners to understand.

A recent *Los Angeles Times* piece suggested humans should get out of the whale captivity business. These animals, like so many animals, need their herd and their freedom. Migration over thousands of miles is built into their biology and their being.

"Killer whales form close-knit, lifelong family groups. They travel long distances in a day and are extremely intelligent. Marine parks are not aquariums that exist to rescue and study animals in humane environments and to educate the public. They are high-profit water circuses in which intelligent ocean predators have been forced into unnatural lives."

The vital role of family and freedom resonates with horse owners. We know that the more space we give our horses, the better off they'll be. And that to be with friends and family is essential.

The more we constrain their movement, the more stressed they'll be. They may not kill us (like captive killer whales have been known to do), but their stress will express itself in stereotypies, raised cortisol levels, abnormal behavior, and physiological issues. And it's the same deal with keeping horses isolated from one another.

These are simple animal priorities. But in our zealous attempts to control them and create human-like living arrangements, we overlook the fact that they are not humans.

With their behavior, 'difficult' horses are simply saying, 'Let me be a horse.'

And the whale is just saying, 'Let me be a whale.'

HORSES SOLVING HORSE PROBLEMS

If you want to measure a horse's smarts, don't give it math problems or ask it to distinguish musical genres. Instead, test its ability to solve horse problems. That's the message from scientist Frans de Waal of Emory University.

Dr. de Waal chastened his peers for anthropomorphism and urged all scientists, equine researchers included, to know their subjects intimately before conducting research. His essay on animal intelligence was published in the *Wall Street Journal*.

For the last two thousand years or so, we've put ourselves at the top of the intelligence tree. Aristotle, Darwin, and others developed an order and rank of all living things. Humans fell just shy of angels.

All the other animals fell below us. All others lacked souls. They were bereft of a sense of identity or a moral, emotional nature. More recently, B.F. Skinner and his followers considered that animals are fairly simple and predictable stimulus-and-response machines.

The intelligence tree is actually more like a brambly, knotty bush. How accurately you measure and define animal intelligence depends on how well you know your subjects.

De Waal writes, "We have grossly underestimated both the scope and the scale of animal intelligence. Experiments with animals have long been handicapped by our anthropocentric attitude: We often test them in ways that work fine with humans but not so well with other species."

Anyone can be blinded by ignorance and hubris; equine researchers are no exception. "Scientists may miss or ignore the small subtleties—things obvious to a horseman," said renowned colt starter Mike Kevil, when I spoke with him a few years back. "If they don't know what it means, it means nothing to them."

De Waal would concur. He writes, "If I walk through a forest... and fail to see or hear the pileated woodpecker, am I permitted to conclude that the bird is absent? Of course not. We know how easily these splendid woodpeckers hop around tree trunks to stay out of sight...Absence of evidence is not evidence of absence."

Picture, for example, a grazing horse. To uninformed observers, it's just grazing. But watch closely and you'll see the horse selecting one grass over another, spitting out unsavory plants. It learns and categorizes smells and forage spots, scans the horizon, registers sounds typical to field and season, and stays mindful of its herd mates.

OR

Picture a horse in a stall. It eats and drinks and moves about. To the uninformed, the horse is fine. But those familiar with wild or unconfined horses may have a different perspective. By comparing behaviors, blood work, and vitals, this horse may be more stressed and less healthy than its unconfined brethren.

What you see or miss in horses depends on perspective and experience. It turns out that Clever Hans couldn't count. But he could read his owner's subtle body language. Does that make him less intelligent than we first believed?

"I would argue that the horse was in fact very smart," says de Waal. "His abilities at arithmetic may have been flawed, but his understanding of human body language was remarkable. And isn't that the skill a horse needs most?"

Along the same lines, who more accurately assesses your nervousness or confidence level—a horse or a fellow human?

Stephen Budiansky, author of *The Nature of Horses*, writes articulately of our biased view of intelligence, "In our culture, we tend to think of an ability to solve problems or to quickly make connections or to assimilate new information as more important signs of intelligence than a good memory (thus the respected absent-minded professor) ...we tend to dismiss innate mental skills from the equation.

"When comparing the intelligence of different species, though, it behooves us...to consider all the functions that an animal's brain is called upon to perform before we pass judgment on its mental ranking in the animal kingdom."

We humans are predators, and we tend to think more highly of fellow predators, posits Budiansky. We'd probably rank those in the dog family, like mice-eating coyotes, above grass-eating horses. He writes, "...Problem solving is part of the survival kit of a [predator] that lives by anticipating the complex and highly varied actions of elusive prey. Mice move and hide, grass doesn't." But learning, Budiansky writes, "...is survival in a changing environment where the rules are not fixed." And horses learn well.

At a clinic in Europe years ago, Leslie Desmond recalled turning about eight horses loose and letting them move around the arena together. Her audience—full of equine researchers, behaviorists, and published authors—was "open-mouthed in disbelief" and told her it was downright dangerous.

"What it showed me was that they didn't really understand that the horse's basic nature is to get along," said Desmond. "My stumbling block regarding equine behavior research coming out of universities and academia is that it seems like they don't know horses as well as good horsemen. One would like to support equine research for the betterment of the species, but it's hard to get behind it when they don't seem to know what they're talking about."

But there's hope. Just as approaches to horsemanship have evolved from domination to partnership, equine researchers are beginning to test horses from horse perspectives.

De Waal writes: "Scientists are now finally meeting animals on their own terms instead of treating them like furry (or feathery) humans, and this shift is fundamentally reshaping our understanding."

BLANKETING

I n a thoroughly researched paper, Natalija Aleksandrova makes a strong, supported argument for not blanketing horses. Ever. Aleksandrova, a horsewoman, hoof trimmer, and equine researcher, posted her essay, which cited twenty scientific references, on the pages of *Academia Liberti*, a school of holistic equine study based in Germany.

She appeals to horse owners to let horses take care of themselves. By blanketing and using other ill-advised horse management techniques, owners inadvertently rob horses of their natural ability to regulate their body temperatures.

The researcher, who lives in Latvia, writes that horses have efficient, multi-faceted thermoregulatory mechanisms. They are perfectly adapted to staying warm all winter, given their anatomy, physiology, and individual and herd behavior. Domestic horses need only conditions that the species should rightly have "by dictate of Nature," she writes. They are:

- Freedom of movement twenty-four hours a day
- Free access to appropriate food (fibrous hay) twenty-four hours a day
- Herd life
- Proper hoof care
- Shelter that it can enter and leave freely

But what about these thermoregulatory mechanisms? Simply put, they're how horses maintain their body temperature. These innate abilities can be broken down categorically:

Anatomy and Physiology

The skin and coat are excellent insulators. In fact, due to horses' anatomy and physiology, it's easier for them to stay warm in cold weather than to stay cool in hot weather or after an intense workout.

Long before the first snow flies, horses naturally grow a winter coat. Coats vary by species and environment, but generally, horses in colder climates have evolved to grow thicker coats. In addition, horses increase the insulating abilities of their coats by as much as 30 percent through piloerection, the raising or lowering of the coat via hair-erector muscles. Blanketing inhibits piloerection.

Horse hair naturally has an oily coating that helps shed rain and snow. Blanketing and over-grooming interfere with this innate, insulating trait. "Needless to say, the popular practice of clipping the hair of a horse's coat eliminates, completely, the thermoregulatory factor of the coat," writes Aleksandrova.

Horses' arteries constrict or dilate, depending on thermoregulatory requirements. Constriction reduces heat loss by reducing the amount of warm blood brought to the cooler body surface (in winter, for instance). Dilation allows for a larger amount of hot blood from overheated interiors to reach the body surface and to be cooled (during or after exercise and in hot environments).

Horses don't hibernate, of course, but they may still add as much as 20 percent body weight in fat as cold weather approaches. That extra layer is important; fat is three times more insulating than other tissues, according to Aleksandrova.

Behavior

Horses may burn off some of that fat to stay warm, but they still need to eat more during winter. The shift is called climatic energy demand, and it increases by about 1 percent for every degree decrease (Celsius). Metabolically, it's essential that horses have ready access to fibrous fuel around the clock. The wood that heats their house is hay.

Wild horses conserve energy by moving less in the winter; so do domestic horses. Horses may stand next to each other or use each other as wind blocks, thus "reducing the body surface area exposed to the environment and gaining heat from a pair or group source," she writes.

Though not quantified by research, Aleksandrova observes that blanketing creates a no-win scenario because the horse cannot heat specific regions of its body: "The whole body cools or the whole body heats up. Sweating under a blanket is more of a problem metabolically to the horse than people realize."

Blanketing forces the entire spectrum of horses' mechanisms to languish. She writes, "They don't need to exercise hair erector muscles, nor to dilate or constrict arteries, nor to activate sweat glands, nor to prepare or deplete healthy fat reserves. All muscles atrophy without exercising for a period of time. Horses under blankets effectively lose their ability to stay warm on their own."

In conclusion, Aleksandrova speculates that other management techniques—"stabling, separating from equine companions, forced exercising, lack of continuous fiber (hay) uptake"—can compound their stress and inability to cope with cold.

Blanketing Sidebar

We'd rather *feel* right than *be* right. After all, having a bunch of people tell us we're right is way better than being told we're wrong. According to Clay Johnson, author of *The Information Diet*, we'd prefer people agree with us even when we're dead wrong.

Imagine then how excited I was to come across:

"Results of a multi-year study by Colorado State University, one of the top equine veterinary schools in the country:

- Blanketing horses is one of the worst things you can do in the winter.
- Horses have the ability to loft and lower their coats... it's like exchanging different blankets all day and night.
- It turns out that blanketing is done more for pleasing the human. The horse blanket industry has done a great job of making us think that their product is a necessary part of good horsekeeping, when it is actually very seldom needed."

I'd hit a gold mine! I went to the Colorado State website and delved into their research archives to confirm my findings. When I came up empty, I wrote to their Equine Science department.

Director Dr. Jerry B. Black responded, "We have investigated all departments and found that no study was conducted here at CSU in any part of the Equine Science program. I am afraid someone has used our name to promote their own opinion. In our investigation, we could not find ANY evidence that there has been a scientific study done on this subject at ANY institution."

Gold mine? How 'bout fool's gold? I'd been juked by someone on my own team. It was a jolting reminder to always double-check my facts and stick as close to the raw data as possible.

In *The Information Diet*, Johnson borrows from Michael Pollan, best-selling author of *The Omnivore's Dilemma* and others, who recommended, "Eat food. Not too much. Mostly plants." When it comes to information, said Johnson in an interview: "Seek. Not too much. Mostly facts."

Don't treat your Facebook news feed as gospel. Like fried dough, it might taste good going down. But I doubt it sits right later.

WHIP USE

The more you use a whip, the less successful you'll be over jumps. But carry one without using it, and you may do better than without one. That's the gist of recent research by Catherine Watkins and Darcy Murphy of Hartpury College in England. Their findings were included in the proceedings of the International Society of Equitation Science Conference recently held in Delaware.

Taken at its most basic, the research correlates nicely with the barrel racing study done by Karen Waite at Michigan State University. She found that aggressive riding (with whipping and spurring) did not make for faster barrel runs and negatively impacted cooperation from horses.

The Watkins-Murphy study looked at about five hundred horse-and-rider pairs in British show jumping at elite and non-elite levels. It found that the likelihood of faults increased with greater whip use. The researchers also discovered that novice riders use and carry whips a bit more than elite riders (a finding noted in the barrel racing study, too).

Sixty-nine percent of novice riders carry whips, compared to 62 percent of elite riders. But the correlation between simply carrying (as opposed to using) a whip and jumping clear rounds shows an interesting element that begs for further study:

- Twenty-three percent of riders carrying but not using a whip had clear rounds.
- Sixteen percent of riders without a whip got a clear round.
- Just 7 percent of whip-using riders got clear rounds.

What gives? Could these results reflect rider confidence or horses knowing of the whip prospect? Future research might test jumping rounds of the same horse and rider pairs with and without whips.

Whips seem to be increasingly viewed as counter-effective by the academic world. Dr. Paul McGreevy and others have shown as much in their investigation of Australian thoroughbred racing. And indications are that the studies may have some impact on the policies related to equine welfare.

For the record, some critics say these researchers are confusing cause with correlation:

- Novice horses need to be reinforced and disciplined with the whip.
- Novice riders need to use aids like whips until they refine their technique.
- When the horses learn and partnerships get better, the whip goes away, critics say.

It'll be interesting to see if the British Showjumping Association amends its rules to deter whip use. Could novice riders become better without them? Would they find another piece of gear to replace it?

What's more important to British Showjumping and its competitors—successful performances or what's best for the horse? At the very least, this British study helps us see that any tool—spurs and whips included—can be abusive or effective. It's up to us as riders to use them appropriately and with respect for the welfare of the horse.

A Whip by Any Other Name – Sidebar

A recent trail incident provided some timely relevance to the discussion of whip use. Comet and I went for a solo trail ride. We got off the road and into the woods only to be bombarded by deer flies.

Since I was a girl, I'd grabbed long twigs as impromptu fly whisks. This ride was no different. I pulled up to a tree and broke off a leafy branch.

Comet was fine with standing still while I snapped off the two-foot length. But it was another story when she saw that I now held a stick-like implement. She spun and fussed and bounced around. I let her move and took some time to show her my intentions.

With the flies as bad as they were, it didn't take long for her to understand. Those gentle, leafy touches on her poll and neck meant relief not punishment.

When we got back home, I talked with Steve, who has owned her for seven years. Before that, he had witnessed her previous owner get after her with a stick. It was just one of several abusive implements the man regularly used. Since then, she hasn't had any such object raised against her.

But horses have a tendency not to forget. Perhaps that should be considered when weighing the effect of whip use and carriage.

BARREL RACING

Graham Motion knows it. Selby Barrett knows it too. A relaxed horse is a fast horse. Motion is the thoroughbred trainer whose Animal Kingdom won the 2011 Kentucky Derby. *The Wall Street Journal* wrote about his unique training methods as they apply to horses and business management. Barrett is the young Mainer excelling at collegiate barrel racing at Murray State University. Their training is geared around this tenet: Relaxed and happy horses do best.

Now researchers at Michigan State University have helped to quantify what these trainers knew empirically: Nothing's gained by forcing or intimidating your horse with whipping or kicking. In fact, there may be a lot to lose. The MSU team led by Karen Waite looked at 'aggressive riding' among barrel racers and referenced previous findings, which showed thoroughbreds raced faster when no whip was used.

Waite and company looked at more than sixty horse-and-rider pairs competing at state level barrel racing competitions. The pairs all raced in the same arena where the footing and race length were the same.

What is aggressive riding? Researchers defined and quantified it by watching what riders were doing to the horses with their legs and hands and distinguishing these actions with labels. They also developed a catalog for horse behaviors that included rearing, tail swishing, and kicking out. Then they timed and videotaped the pairs. Lo and behold: whipping and spurring did not make for faster runs. It did, however, make for less cooperative pairs. Horses with aggressive riders had more issues entering the arena, and tended to buck and rear more often.

Great news from an exemplary study; researchers get high marks for its simplicity and approach. Motion, the thoroughbred trainer, said, "If horses are very nervous or wound up, they're not going to race well because they're running on nervous energy." His sentiment reflects what we know about a horse's sympathetic (fight or flight) versus its parasympathetic (rest and digest) nervous system. We want them to be interested and engaged, not frightened.

ACUPUNCTURE

It was not a Kodak moment for acupuncture. Dr. Cynthia Reynolds was working at an Arizona racetrack in the late 1990s. She watched as a colleague tried treating a colicky horse with acupuncture, inserting thin needles through his skin. "The horse just dropped," recalled Reynolds. "He got dramatically worse."

Reynolds saw first-hand the impact this traditional Chinese treatment can have on a horse. The incident helped propel her on an educational journey that has ultimately led her to becoming the most prominent veterinarian acupuncturist in Maine. (Thankfully, the horse fully recovered.)

At Thanksgiving Farm in Durham, Maine, the horses have benefited from Reynolds's treatment for years: "Her visits are not only welcomed by us but by our animals," said owner Barbara Stanley. "They do not react to her with fear but with curiosity and anticipation. They seem to recognize Vet Cindy as the one that makes them feel better, which certainly gives us all peace of mind."

Just as *feng shui* has worked its way into design, so too has acupuncture grown from its Chinese roots into the equine veterinary practice. Most of us horse owners don't really understand the concept, but if it can make our horses feel better, why not go with it?

Feng shui and acupuncture both address *Qi*, pronounced 'chee.' Translated literally from Mandarin Chinese, Qi means 'air' or 'breath.' But it is more accurately defined as a life force or energy flow. When flow is disrupted, imbalances develop and the body becomes compromised. Acupuncture seeks to restore proper flow; needles help free up blockages.

I spoke with Dr. Reynolds and Dr. Matt Randall, a vet and acupuncturist in Texas. Acupuncture is best used to treat chronic pain, lameness, and allergies, they told me. Randall said it has also has been effective in treating anhidrosis (an inability to sweat) and heaves.

Many practitioners, including Reynolds and Randall, often use it in conjunction with chiropractic treatment. It works. But how?

How do Western-trained scientists design a research project using the scientific method to test and quantify such a mystical energy? It seems a bit like asking a Grand Prix rider to go rope some cattle where his ingrained skills and perspective might make the task more challenging than if he was starting with no skills or viewpoint at all. It's a bit like quantifying a horseman's 'feel' with units of measurement like seconds and ounces.

Some vets, including Dr. David Ramey, have suggested that horses get similarly positive results from placebo acupuncture.

Indeed, said Randall, many experiments have produced unconvincing results because researchers have poorly defined a proper placebo or control group. Would horses in the control group get no needles? Would they get needles placed away from Qi pathways? Randomly-placed needles? Those needles may still end up near acupoints and end up eliciting a response, said Randall.

The University of Florida's Dr. Huisheng Xie and colleagues have done the bulk of research quantifying acupuncture's effects. In an experiment which echoes what Reynolds saw on the Arizona track, researchers have shown that colic can be induced through acupuncture. (Yes, horses get colic and mice get cancer. All in the name of science.)

A more beneficent project has shown that more of the body's natural painkillers (endorphins, serotonin, norephinephrine, and gamma-aminobutyric acid) are released when acupuncture needles are effectively placed. While the research may be equivocal, anecdotal evidence is quite positive. "The licking and chewing is our key that we've done something that's making the horse feel better," said Randall.

Acupuncture helps by reducing the amount of medication, including artificial painkillers and steroids, and by reducing lameness, he added. "Horses are better quicker."

Considering scientists' fixed parameters, it seems likely that researchers may be looking at acupuncture from the wrong angle. Future experiments might yield more conclusive results if new perspectives and different measurements were observed.

Our traditional Western work-up, for instance, yields a physical exam, blood work, biochemistry, x-rays, etc. By all these measurements, a horse might be fine, but given the traditional Chinese evaluation, that same 'well' horse might reveal pathologies.

Randall advocates both Western and Eastern medicine. "Using the two modalities will get you better results. They're synergistic. They work better together than either by themselves," he said.

Randall and Reynolds cautioned clients when NOT to treat with acupuncture: Pregnant mares, horses with cancer ("You don't want to give tumors energy," said Randall.), and at certain times when steroids are in use, since steroids suppress the immune system and needles may infrequently introduce infection.

Reynolds always relies on an experienced handler to assist during treatment. In most cases, it's Moore. "I'd much prefer having him there for safety. That way I'm confident about who's handling the horse. He's a big asset," she said.

SOUND STUDIES NOT SO SOUND

Voice

Researchers are starting to examine voice and its impact on equine behavior. They ask: When you talk with your horse, does he listen?

In one study at Nottingham Trent University, researchers identified voice as a 'modality' or a way in which we communicate a command. Other modalities could be visual (waving a hand or flag) or tactile (direct pressure on the mouth, side, seat, etc.). Researchers studied twenty horses as they worked on transitions from a stop to walk, walk to trot, and then those same transitions in reverse. In other words, does your voice make any difference when asking a horse to speed up or slow down?

They found that horses directed by more than one modality (bit pressure and voice cues) catch on more quickly at first. But as training continues, researchers found horses do just as well without the voice modality. Voice cues, we are led to believe, could be ineffective and unnecessary.

In another study, scientists from Delaware, Michigan, Germany, and Italy collaborated to test the effect of harsh versus soft voice tones when asking a horse to cross a tarp. They found it doesn't matter which tone is used. A horse, they write, doesn't inherently understand the difference between harsh and soft tones. There's no correlation between tarp-crossing success and voice tones. Nor is there any correlation between stress (as measured by heart rate) and voice tones.

These scientific efforts make sense and are fine contributions to our horse knowledge, especially if considered in concert with our own experiences and observations. We know, for instance, that wild horses learn to associate sounds with good or bad consequences through direct experience or through the reaction of their herd mates. (Think of predator sounds, storm sounds, flowing water sounds, etc.)

You'll see that in domestic life, horses quickly learn that a lot of sounds don't matter at all and have no impact on their well-being. (Think of passing garbage trucks, on-site construction noise, screaming kids passing by.)

But, of course, as horse owners, we know voice or sound matter if part of a regime. Horses can learn to associate it with the more direct cues of pressure and release. Or even simple cause and effect, like when you call them in from the pasture for feed.

The Nottingham Trent University researchers eliminated the voice cue. But what would have happened if they had eliminated the bit pressure instead?

For what they were really testing, if you read their report, is multi-modality versus single-modality learning. In other words, teaching a horse with a combination of cues, then gradually eliminating some to refine the message. Well-trained horses learn to react to cues that are more and more subtle.

At my barn, for example, every cue but the voice has been eliminated in some situations. When doing ground work, my horses learn to associate the "Tssst!" sound with a quick pressure asking them to back off. (It could be backing off feed, another horse, or an open gate.)

Hundreds of times, they have heard "Tssst," quickly followed by the light pressure of the lead line, asking them to step back. By now, they no longer require tactile pressure to respond. A "Tssst' is enough.

Another example of an effective audible cue is the big sigh. I let it out when I want my horse to slow down. Initially, she heard my sigh in conjunction with a more relaxed, less forward body position, plus the touch of a rein. Now, she'll slow down when I sigh.

Nonetheless, voice cues are harder to pass on consistently from one rider to the next than rein pressure or leg pressure. That might explain why most accomplished trainers don't use them.

A Canine Sidebar on Voice Cues

Belle is about eight years old. For the first year, I could say the word "walk" without consequence. But after a while, she connected the word with a really good time. Saying 'walk' whipped her up. She'd bark and spin around, desperate to get started.

To avoid the circus, I started spelling it out when I needed to tell family where I was headed. Now, she recognizes the spelling. Does that mean she's learned to spell?

Music

Dogs love *Downton Abbey*. It's true. My dog watches it with me every week. That's far-fetched reasoning, of course, drawn up by much subjectivity and human interpretation. And it reminds me of two recent studies on music and horse behavior.

A group at the University of Queensland, Australia, played the *Forrest Gump* theme song for six weanlings all day and compared their heart rates to un-*Gumped* weanlings. Another study at Hartpury College in England, compared the behavior of eight geldings when exposed to periods of jazz, classical, country, and rock.

The scientists get kudos for taking some compelling first steps to document horse behavior as it relates to music. Both acknowledge that further studies will help elucidate the ways in which horses may benefit from auditory experiences. Hats off for these initial, albeit small-sized, studies.

But before researchers plan follow-up studies, let's consider filling in some holes of reasoning and viewing the larger question of how sound, not music, affects horses.

We humans recognize music as one kind of sound. We know it has melody, harmony, and rhythm. Music varies by its timbre, key (major or minor), instrumentation (voice, horns, strings, etc.), and percussive effect. Through our upbringing and social interactions, we've learned to quantify music as soothing, rambunctious, mellow, or unnerving. Each of these qualifiers varies from person to person, family to family, culture to culture.

I love country. My kids don't. Bolliwood radio is big in India. Not here.

How do we know horses can differentiate music from sound or noise? Both studies seem to make this presumption. It's a cart-before-the-horse kind of flaw.

In the Queensland study, researchers put stallions next to the weanlings with the knowledge that studs tend to rile up the babies. They found that playing music decreased the time a weanlings' pulse was elevated with stallions near. Their control was no music. As in no recorded sound.

But what if playing *Forrest Gump* simply drowned out other noises that might have aroused the young horses if only they heard them? Would white noise, dolphin calls, or fax machine screeches have had the same positive impact?

Before we conclude that music soothes horses' souls, we might examine the more general impact of noise on heart rate. We may find, for example, that any sound that minimizes or drowns out the various intimidating stallion sounds will benefit the young 'uns.

In the Hartpury study, a catalog of equine behaviors, ranging from relaxed to stressed, substituted for heart-rate monitoring as indicators of their horses' well-being. According to their behavior catalog or ethogram, Hartpury horses got jazzed up by jazz but acted more restful with classical and country.

Most of us humans can distinguish musical genres. Horses cannot.

Before researchers dive into what kind of country music horses prefer, let's find out if they act more relaxed or jazzed by white noise or talk radio.

To their credit, the Hartpury researchers hinted at possible attributes for calm or excitatory music (namely, tempo and key). But to say that horses are better off listening to country music is misleading, since we can find slow songs, fast songs, sharp songs, and flat songs within any genre, country included.

Hartpury, by the way, selected Hank Williams.

Back to my dog and *Downton Abbey*, it is true that she lies down beside me and watches it. She appears happy and at peace. But does she just like lying next to me? Is she feeding off my own behavior of restful contentment? Did she see a dog or hear a bark on TV once and is waiting to see or hear it again? Does the TV emit nice sounds that only dogs can hear? To say she likes *Downton Abbey* is simply skipping past all these possibly more plausible notions. Sound familiar?

SUPPLEMENTS

"It may be that the best supplement is no supplement at all. Avoiding spending money on supplements is particularly appropriate for horse owners struggling to simply maintain their horses in this difficult economy. No benefit is achieved with hypernutrition," writes researcher Dr. David Ramey.

Ah, the wizards of marketing! They've convinced us we should give our kids vitamins. I'm not talking about toddlers and Flintstones. I'm talking about the billion-dollar industry that is horse supplements. As horse owners, many of us think we need to add vitamins, minerals, herbs, and chemicals to our horses' diet.

But Ramey says it ain't so. He researched supplements and recently presented his findings to the American Association of Equine Practitioners. He writes, "Based on my analysis, if you're giving your horse enough alfalfa or grass hay, so he can keep his weight, he's getting pretty much 100 percent of what he needs."

Ramey's only caveat is to offer horses a salt block and consider selenium if you live in areas deficient in that mineral (much of the eastern United States, for instance). If you think of horses' big picture evolutionarily, Ramey's conclusion should come as no surprise. For thousands of years, they did just fine without us, without stuff.

Ramey's second element of his research was to analyze the supplements. He found them woefully lacking. Not only do they lack balance (oversupplying one nutritional need while offering no supply of others) but often the labels misrepresented actual contents. He calls supplement use a kind of "nutritional roulette."

Whatever the term, it's clear you're not doing your horse any favors, and you're not doing your wallet any favors, either.

DEWORMING

The days of deworming every other month are over. Research shows that you do more harm than good when you order that annual variety pack and stuff worming paste down your horse's throat indiscriminately. Why?

Most horses don't need wormer and by giving it to them anyway, you lower their resistance. On average, just one horse in a herd of four hosts the majority of parasites. That horse should be identified and treated accordingly.

Today's body of evidence points to the importance of doing annual or spring/fall fecal egg counts to pinpoint the specific horse, the specific parasites, and direct treatment. It's been called 'targeted worming.'

"The object of targeted worming is to cut way back on the amount of worm medicine being used and so lessen the ability of the parasites to develop immunity to it. It's similar to human medicine where your doctor doesn't want to give you antibiotics for every little infection," writes Dr. Dave Jefferson of Maine Equine Associates.

Think about it. We wouldn't give our kids amoxicillin every January, just cuz. It would be absurd and harmful. That kind of pointless medication would eventually render amoxicillin useless because, over time, bacteria would morph into new amoxicillin-resistant bacteria.

Jefferson recommends regular fecal egg counts. His practice does them in-house. Even with the cost, Jefferson says clients save money by not using wormers so often. And the horses are healthier for it. Of course, there's the added bonus of knowing exactly which horse has parasites and which parasites need targeting.

More information. Less blind treatment. Sound good?

HORSENALITY

Pat and Linda Parelli have introduced millions to safe and effective methods for working with horses. Their clinics and DVDs have given us easy-to-grasp tools for better horse-human relationships and horse handling. Their marketing is slicker than their skills, but who cares as long as the horse isn't hurt. But when they start talking nonsense, I take issue. And Horsenality is pure nonsense.

I watched the DVD in which Linda discusses extroverts, introverts, left-brained, and right-brained horses. She refers to a complicated, multi-colored, cylindrical chart. She encourages us to map our horses. It was confusing as heck.

Research her terms and you will quickly discover that Parelli has horse-ified the popular Myers Briggs Personality Indicator. The MBPI is a pop psychology test for humans, used for decades to determine how you might fit into a workplace or behave in a team environment, etc. The women who developed it were not scientists. It has no scientific basis and has been widely critiqued as an ineffective testing tool.

Now comes Linda Parelli and the Parelli School of Horsemanship. Parelli converts a bogus people-personality test for use on horses.

I suppose Horsenality might have some traction if horses had human brains. But really. Horses are no more capable of being 'introverted' than we are capable of grazing on grass all day.

In essence, the Parellis are encouraging us to relate to horses as we would other humans. "This approach to understanding horses helps horses—and their humans—become more balanced, centered and confident."

But horses are by nature balanced and centered. Considering horses as horses is what we need to do. First. Last. Always.

I love science, and I would welcome real science-based horse training by the Parellis.

Addendum

Clinton Anderson is equally guilty of presenting false science in his program. He refers to 'the thinking side of the brain' versus 'the reactive side of the brain.'

He might have the right idea. Horses have a flight instinct when their sympathetic nervous system is engaged. That's reactive alright. Alternatively, they may appear to be thinking when they're relaxed and their parasympathetic nervous system takes over.

But introducing terms like 'thinking side' and 'reactive side' is flat out wrong. If Clinton studied the autonomic nervous system of the horse, he could present a more accurate picture.

GROOMING

On a recent day trip, we pulled our trailer up to a few other ones in a big parking lot. Several ladies were diligently grooming their horses. We saddled up and headed out on the trail. The ladies were still grooming their horses. Or trying. We watched as the horses stepped from side to side and whinnied at us. I started thinking about the pros and cons of grooming. It turns out there aren't many pros:

- Yes, it's good to put hands on your horse so you're aware of any nicks, scratches, or swellings.
- Yes, it's good to check their feet daily.

But there are plenty of cons. That might explain why prominent horsemen and women have so little to say about grooming. It might explain, too, why working cowboys typically clean the saddle area, check horses' feet, and call it good.

Here's a sampling of how grooming can be detrimental:

- Vibrissae or whisker trimming can lead to injury. Each of those whiskers has its own nerve. Horses use their whiskers like we use fingers, to feel an object, a food item, another horse.
- Feathers and fetlock hair helps shed water, according to Dr. Stephanie Larson, of Abraham's Equine Clinic in Cedar Rapids, Iowa. Trimming them can lead to potential hoof problems as moisture from dew or rain collects there instead of shedding off.
- Excessive bathing and sheath cleaning can lead to dermatological issues, said Larson.
- Grooming products aren't cheap.

So why groom? Grooming is great if you are unable to ride. The horses look nicer, and it provides us humans with feel-good moments.

I'm all for a clean horse. But when you consider grooming, don't assume you're doing your horse any favors. Those horses in the parking lot clearly would have preferred to be moving out on the trail.

RIDER WEIGHT

Say a prayer for the chair. That's what some waitresses glibly say when seating a heavy diner. Now equine research is telling us to say a prayer for the pony. Or better yet, bring in the Percheron.

Dr. Hayley Randle and colleagues published their findings in *The Journal of Veterinary Behavior*. They studied over one hundred fifty riders across England and found that only 5 percent fell within British equine vet guidelines for rider-to-horse weight ratio (10 percent of horse weight).

The United States ranks significantly higher than England in obesity statistics. And by extension, one can conclude it has more overweight riders. The study reasons, therefore, that the problem must be comparably worse for American horses. (Interestingly enough, American guidelines allow for a higher rider-to-horse weight ratio, varying from 15–20 percent of horse weight.)

Randle is among a growing number of scientists suggesting that the human obesity problem can create a wide spectrum of issues for horses, including but not limited to lameness, back pain, and behavioral problems (bucking, rearing, not following commands). "People tend to think horses are such big animals, they must be okay, and not to take notice of the weight issue. But the health impact on the horse can be quite extreme, quite quickly," Dr. Randle told *The Daily Mail*.

The finding verifies what many clinicians are seeing in arenas, especially where it impacts horsemanship skills and the horse-rider partnership. "A rider that is not fit or not balanced is likely to misuse the reins or the saddle horn for balance," said horsewoman Leslie Desmond. "Riders who are overweight and out of shape will compromise a horse."

Horseman Jeff Griffith led a colt-starting clinic at the Iowa Equestrian Center. Nearly all of the fifteen college-age students were overweight and needed mounting blocks to get on their horses. "I hate mounting blocks," he told the group. "If you are reasonable with your height, get on your horse! Keep getting on your horse off the ground. It might come in handy some day."

So what do you do if you're too heavy for your horse? There are two ways to change the ratio: Ride a bigger horse or lose weight. Or, as both scientists and clinicians suggest, consider driving a cart instead of climbing into the saddle.

Weight Does Matter – Sidebar

Together with the horse, we're Olympians. Together, we're scholarship athletes. We're a legendary duo, crossing continents, scaling mountains, swimming rivers, and out-sprinting nearly every other species on the planet.

But somewhere along the line, it became OK to partner-up with our horses as overweight, out-of-shape humans. Increasingly, the horse community seems to give heavy riders a free pass, an enthusiastic blessing even. We don't hurt feelings. It's more important that we ride well and treat our horses nicely. Who cares if we're heavy?

Certainly, rider weight shouldn't overshadow the need to have lightness, balance, and a proper fitting saddle. But for the sake of a reasonable discussion on rider weight, let's assume those variables are controlled.

Take two riders with equal balance, lightness of feel, and properly-fitting saddles. Would the horse do better with a one-hundred-pound partner or a two-hundred-pound partner?

Clinicians are worried. They see more and more riders compromising their ability because they're overweight and unfit. They worry these riders won't be handy getting out of a jam. They worry about the horses.

It's time we reconsidered ourselves as athletes and athletic partners. The only successful heavy athletes I've seen lately are golfers, bowlers, and the occasional relief pitcher. Riding requires significantly more effort, agility and athleticism than swinging at or throwing a ball. Heavy athletes are most certainly rejected from other sports where lifting or carrying them is required (figure skating, ballroom dancing).

All other things being equal, let's think about our weight and how it impacts our horses, say nothing for our safety and ability to be agile in the saddle. Admitting the problem can be the first step in remedying it.

LYME DISEASE

Lyme disease cycle in bug terms: egg, larva, nymph, adult, repeat. Lyme disease cycle in horse owner terms: pain, expense, frustration, confusion, repeat. It's hard to believe such a tiny organism (*Borrelia burdorferi*), hosted by a larger but still tiny organism (deer tick), could wreak such havoc on the welfare of our horses and our wallets.

Available information is conflicting and sometimes hard to interpret, but consider yourself lucky. Thirty years after its discovery, treatment and testing options are exponentially better than they were in the 1980s. Today, we have options. Unfortunately, none of them are cheap.

First, a little immunology primer: When an animal gets an infection, the body mounts a defense by producing proteins called antibodies. They are responding to the bacteria or antigen. So, tests for diseases typically measure the presence of either antibodies or antigens.

When Lyme is suspected (due to soreness or obvious tick exposure), most vets draw blood and send it to Cornell University or the University of Connecticut. Cornell is home to Animal Health

Diagnostic Center. UConn has the Connecticut Veterinary Medical Diagnostic Laboratory.

In 2011 Cornell introduced the new Multiplex test that can reportedly identify the infection's stage. The CVMDL administers the Western Blot test, which identifies more antibodies than the Multiplex test but is reportedly not as accurate at pinpointing the stage.

Each year, Cornell and UConn labs process tens of thousands of blood samples for Lyme disease. CVMDL ran five thousand samples last year (at about $60 per sample). Vets will charge between $100 to $170 for drawing the blood, sending off the sample, and then consulting on the results.

But some vets are starting to use a new test, SNAP 4Dx Plus, which can be done right in the stall. The test was originally made for dogs by IDEXX Laboratories, a Maine company. Unlike the Western Blot or Multiplex, the SNAP test doesn't quantify the presence of Lyme disease in your horse's blood. It just tells you if it's there.

Dr. Marc Reilly of South Shore Equine in Plympton, Massachusetts, compared it to a human pregnancy test: It's simple and super accurate. "If it's positive, it's positive," said Reilly. His practice has tested over a thousand horses in the area south of Boston, toward Cape Cod. Four hundred have been treated for Lyme.

Before the SNAP test came along, most dog vets sent blood work out to labs for testing, just like horse vets do now. "It was expensive and time-consuming," said Dr. Gene Szymkowiak of the Coralville (Iowa) Animal Hospital. He's used the SNAP test for two years.

The IDEXX test is cheaper and quicker than the Western Blot or Multiplex tests and may be the preferred method moving forward since many horse owners don't need to know exactly how badly their horses have Lyme, just like a woman doesn't need to know how pregnant she is. A yes or no will do. (The SNAP also tests for anaplasmosis, another tick-borne disease.)

So your horse has Lyme. What next? Most vets suggest a thirty- to forty-five-day course of the oral antibiotic, doxycycline. It costs over $300 per horse.

Doxy isn't always effective. You may have to use it for longer stretches or return to it after retesting. In addition, doxy has some anti-inflammatory properties (Indeed, some vets give doxy for swelling or soreness when bute or banamine is not an option.) so you may notice improvement, but it won't be because you tackled the infection.

What's more? There have been doxycycline shortages recently. Clients may have to wait for weeks just to start treatment, said Vicki Coffin, at Equine Veterinary Services in Freeport, Maine.

Reilly, of South Shore Equine, prefers treating intravenously with oxytetracycline for a short course, followed by oral oxy. It's twice as effective as using doxy, his research shows. And more expensive.

Dr. Rachel Flaherty of Back Cove Equine in Portland, Maine, typically treats with doxy for forty-two days.

By the way, Ledum is a popular herbal remedy; it may help with symptoms but won't kill the bug.

There are a lot of opinions, interested parties, and fees. But there seems to be at least one point of consensus: Catch it early and treat it.

While it's tempting to wait for symptoms, studies show the longer you wait, the harder it'll be to get rid of the bug. Think of the Borrelia burdorferi as a burrowing little critter who likes to hide. The more time you give it, the longer it'll take to hunt it down. As months go by, the corkscrew-shaped-bacteria will worm its way from bloodstream to joints and bones and even nerves.

"Most horses that are infected don't show it," said Dr. Sandra Bushmich, CVMDL director, who noted that Western Blot detects antibodies about a month after the suspected infection. "If you treat it right then, you have a pretty good chance of getting rid of the infection."

When you're finished with treatment, you still may not be out of the woods. Some vets recommended retesting. Bushmich's lab stores results so clients can monitor recovery, response to treatment, and potential re-infection.

Flaherty doesn't retest. "Even though you won't see improvement with antibody levels, the horse will be better after treatment," she said. Owners get confused by the lack of correlation between numbers and symptoms.

Reilly just does another in-stall SNAP test to check horses' response to treatment.

Some final suggestions:

Lyme disease spreads through its hosts (ticks on deer, possum, and other animals) from New England to west of the Mississippi. Ticks like temperate, moist climates, so Lyme does, too.

But ticks don't like permethrin, vigilance, or dry environments. So using bug spray and checking your horse for ticks are key preventive measures. Moving to New Mexico would help too.

The northeastern United States has endemic areas where the people, dogs, and horses all have Lyme and have responded to it with varying success. If you're bringing horses from an area where there isn't a lot of Lyme, their immune systems will be naive. Flaherty strongly recommends vaccinating those horses.

Coffin, the veteran vet tech, said she was amazed by how dramatically the bug has impacted our area and our horses. "Back when we started testing, a positive horse was unusual. Now a negative horse is very rare."

Lyme Disease – Sidebar I

Researching the Lyme article provided some new perspective into how the animal science business at universities is still a business, and how beating down the disease can have a crippling side effect.

First, the business side effect: Cornell and UConn are obviously affiliated with their labs, the Animal Health Diagnostic Center and the Connecticut Veterinary Medical Diagnostic Laboratory, respectively. AHDC has the Multiplex test; CVMDL does the Western Blot. We hear about pros and cons of one over the other, but both firms agree getting specific antibody levels is crucial. But is it? Sounds irreverent and wrongheaded, I know.

As consumers, we tend to hold universities and their labs beyond reproach. But Dr. Mark Reilly mentioned said that these labs have a vested interest in making money by running tests, even when it might not be the most economical, expedient, or pragmatic diagnostic tool. "It's hard to understand that people in the Ivory Towers would never have a conflict of interest," he said, "but they do."

IDEXX Laboratories, a public company traded on NASDAQ, has a SNAP test that simply gives you a yea or nay on Lyme. Reilly uses it, treats accordingly, and then uses it again to test the antibiotics' effectiveness. The program, he says, works better than the more laborious, conventional testing. "My practice is evidence-based," said Reilly. "The evidence is there. You have to be willing to read it."

Lyme Disease – Sidebar II

CVMDL Director Sandy Bushmich reminded me of a rare phenomenon affecting about 1 percent of Lyme equine patients—the Herxheimer effect, named after Karl Herxheimer, a German doctor who discovered it while developing a treatment for syphilis before Nazis murdered him).

Herx-ing happens when the antibiotics do their job and kill off lots of the targeted bacteria. (In Lyme cases, this would be Borrelia burdorferi.) But then the bug die-off has a toxic impact. The waste-eliminating organs (kidney, liver) have to work overtime to rid the body of the die-off and detoxify. In humans, patients feel crappy, with bad headaches and flu-like symptoms. They feel even worse than they felt before being treated.

In horses, a Herxheimer reaction will be similar to humans, but it can have a potentially devastating effect on the laminae, the tiny features that secure the coffin bone to the hoof wall. When they swell or become irritated, all hell breaks loose. If these comb-like structures get really inflamed, the coffin bone will separate from the hoof wall.

That's founder. No one wants a foundered horse.

Monitoring your horse as it responds to treatment is vital, Bushmich said.

TEN:
Opinions

TRADITIONAL OR PROGRESSIVE?

Look at a typical horseman or woman today. You'll see the outfit isn't a whole lot different from generations past. The jeans, button-down shirt, boots, and hat haven't strayed far from their frontier roots. It's only when you look in the jeans' back pocket, that you might see something new. There's a smartphone.

We're at a special time in the horse world. The past has given us an inspiring legacy of horsemanship and management. The present gives us access to the latest and greatest of virtually every aspect of horse work.

Are you a traditionalist? Or, are you always on the look out for new options?

Many say in today's world that you can follow tradition AND be progressive. In fact, staying true to your roots while being open to new insights might just optimize your horsemanship skills.

"I'm not a school kid, but I love learning," said horseman Mike Kevil, who has equal measures of skepticism and curiosity when it comes to new findings. Whether he's considering a fellow horseman or a science review, Kevil likes to scrutinize beyond the flashy headlines. "Tell me. But tell me *why*. If I don't know the why, I won't apply it the right way. When you know the why, it gets exciting. That's when the learning takes off."

Randy Rieman might agree. He's another horseman who's excelled by respecting tradition while allowing room for new ideas. "The best horsemen are humble, open-minded, and intelligent," said Rieman of his peers. "They're the best because they are consummate learners."

But how do you know where to go when the volume of data is overwhelming? What do you believe when the boldest information isn't always the most reliable?

Academic research can be difficult to find and harder to understand. And great horsemanship often flies under the radar of your typical Google search. Information on the Internet is like that table full of magazines in a doctor's waiting room. Most folks will thumb through entertainment magazines and look at pictures. Those magazines, regardless of their real worth, stay on top. Medical journals, which just might give patients the enlightenment they were looking for, remain buried and unread.

The scientific, which involves forming a hypothesis, gathering and evaluating data and producing results, is not an easy concept to grasp. Better-marketed options may get more attention, not because they're correct, but because people are hired to make them easier to understand, more appealing, sexier.

The Internet has allowed us to self-educate, but results have been mixed. When he first started his equine veterinary practice twenty-four years ago, Dr. Charles Abraham said his clients "didn't have a dang clue about anything." Now, said the Iowa vet, "about 75 percent of them are pretty well educated. It's really made a huge difference."

But self-education comes with pitfalls too. Clients sometimes panic after plugging in their horses' symptoms and confirming worst case scenarios. Others try do-it-yourself diagnosis and get things horribly wrong. "We get a lot more panic calls than we used to. And some clients have a false feeling of being able to diagnose and treat on their own," said Abraham.

Learning how to discriminate between good and bad information isn't hard. Start by educating yourself for real. At Colorado State University, for instance, students build strong science and business foundations to go along with their horsemanship skills before they graduate. "We emphasize the blend of science and industry," said Dr. Jerry B. Black, CSU's Wagonhound Land & Livestock chair in Equine Sciences. "That's how our students hopefully will be future leaders."

In today's world, being well versed in horse sense AND science can be invaluable. Dr. Rebecca Gimenez discovered this the hard way. She was in her early twenties, had grown up with horses, and thought she knew everything. Then, she enrolled in a correspondence course offered by the University of Kentucky. "I didn't recognize half the words in the first paragraph," recalled Gimenez, who now has a PhD in equine science and is president of Technical Large Animal Emergency Rescue, Inc. (TLAER). "I thought, 'How can I not know all this?' I've had horses all my life!"

Now on the other side of the fence, Gimenez sees how handicapped one can be without that science background. "People are intimidated by research," said Gimenez. "It's much easier to listen to quacks. They're better at selling, but none of their crap has ever been exposed to any rigorous scientific evaluation."

Kevil, for one, gravitates toward the brass tacks and challenges of science. "I never feel like I have a complete grasp of it, but I'm curious and want to keep progressing," he said. "I have to read it several times. I lack the vocabulary these researchers use and might need veterinarians to explain it to me in laymen's terms."

Horses can be examined on many levels, from cellular to environmental. If it needs a microscope or an x-ray, you'll need the expertise that goes with the equipment. Be wary of the trainer who claims to know the horse's chemistry if he's never taken a chemistry class.

On the flip side, talented horsemen and women may have the edge over scientists when it comes to behavior or common horse sense. The best can read everything from herd movement to tail swishing and make quick assessments based on experiences with hundreds, if not thousands of interactions. "Scientists may miss or ignore the small subtleties, what would be obvious to a horseman," said Kevil. "If you don't know what it means, it means nothing."

Whether it's sense or science, it pays to get as close to the source as possible. On the Internet, this may mean going to the research, not someone's biased interpretation of the research. On the ground, it means personal experience. Or, as Kevil said, "You have to go and see for yourself."

Bryan Neubert got lucky in this vein. He lived right next to Tom Dorrance. He happened upon work with Ray Hunt and Bill Dorrance, too. "I didn't know they were gifted. But I knew they knew more than I did," said Neubert. "In hindsight, I was extremely blessed. I couldn't have been in a better place anywhere."

Back then, 'clinician' was a new concept and the Internet hardly existed. "I thought a 'clinic' had something to do with a hospital," recalled Neubert with a laugh.

Where would Tom Dorrance have ended up on the proverbial waiting room tabletop? Would you have dug deep to find him?

How we shape our future and our horses' future will be decided, in part, by how well we dig through the waiting room selection and whether we know enough to ask the right questions when we finally see the doctor.

PHOENIX, LIFE & DEATH

Phoenix, my dear paint, was thirty. As she aged, it was increasingly challenging to keep weight on her and take care of her within my means. Giving her every supplement on the planet and swaddling her with constant care were not feasible options.

Mine, like any other, was a personal journey and dilemma. But the other night, as I came in teary-eyed from the barn, I realized writing about it and putting it out there for discussion was something I should do.

So, with a box of Kleenex and a cooling cup of coffee, here goes. Phoenix quid most of her hay and grass. Three times a day, she got a ton of soaked beet pulp and alfalfa pellets added to her complete senior feed and Cocosoya oil. She got forage too.

Most days, she stood in her stall while the others grazed.

I noticed her hanging her head low for long periods of time. When we ponied across the street, she moved slower and slower. She didn't seem to be having much fun anymore. And it wasn't because she was starving.

Sometimes the quality of life question is an easy call—suffering is obvious, with no good end in sight.

But what about Phoenix?

I went to a funeral recently, and the son of the deceased praised her for the very clear wishes she had put down on paper before she had her terrible stroke. When it came time to disconnect life support systems, there was no question of what she would have wanted. "It's never easy," he said, "but with those documents in front of us, it took our self-doubt away. In essence, it had been her decision, not ours. We knew we were doing the right thing."

If only I could have sat down with Phoenix and planned for the end. We do the best we can. We try to be good leaders.

In the wild, of course, there'd be no mercy, no conversation. The herd would have dealt with it one way or another—by leaving her behind, by bullying her further into starvation.

I saw similar behaviors at my barn. At her prime, Phoenix would have a curled lip for anyone who dared come close when she ate. But as she aged, her status dropped from Number 1 to Number 3 out of 4. I closed Phoenix in her stall so she could eat in peace.

How well a domestic horse does, how healthy she stays, how long she lives aren't things she can control. We make the difference between happy, productive lives or sedentary, unhealthy ones. We can make the difference between life and death for a horse. That's the heavy blessing of horse ownership.

I made the dreaded call to my longtime friend and veterinarian, Dr. Linda Barton. The actual process—from administering the shots to burying her—was awful. All the credit is due to vets like Linda who must be there time after time.

We don't think about death when we acquire our animals. On that decided day, all the joys and routines of her life seemed crushed by the weight of that cruel moment.

And now that she's gone, I am trying to overlook those ugly minutes and focus on happy, richer times. That's what Phoenix did. She enriched my life. I tried to tell her 'thank you.'

Like many horses along the way, Phoenix taught me more than I taught her. She taught me that constant pressure on her mouth was counterproductive. She told me she didn't need inch-by-inch direction when bushwhacking through the woods; a gentle neck rein to guide her in a general direction would be fine. She would deal with the finer details, thank you very much. She was a no-nonsense kind of girl when I first met her and remained so until her passing. She was not terribly affectionate but dependable and loyal. We had a wonderfully clear line of communication.

Rest in Peace, Phoenix, with as much grass and sun as you can manage!

MUSTANG POLICY

Talking about mustang policy is like discussing presidential candidates. Most of us sit passionately in one camp or the other. Hard-checked facts are scarce. There's a lot at stake.

Since 1971, the Bureau of Land Management has tried and failed to protect and control the wild horse and burro population. On top of that, the agency's murky, shifting policies have frustrated and dissatisfied stakeholders. Ranchers claim the BLM kowtows to bleeding-heart horse lovers; wild horse advocates say the BLM is beholden to Big Beef.

Stuck in the middle, pleasing no one, and running up an incredible taxpayer tab, the BLM waved a white flag a few years ago. It commissioned the National Academy of Sciences to review its management plan.

I'm thrilled that science and evidence-based collaboration might finally influence policy and enlighten the public in this realm.

Some highlights:

Appropriate Management Levels (AMLs) are at the root of the problem. The BLM develops AMLs in declared Herd Management Areas (HMAs). AMLs are the quota of horses and burros allowed in each area. If the BLM count exceeds the quota, they conduct a roundup. But this practice is flawed on many levels, says the report. "How AMLs are established, monitored, and adjusted is not transparent to stakeholders, supported by scientific information, or amenable to adaptation with new information, environmental and social change.

"Research suggests that transparency is an important contributor to the development of trust between agencies and stakeholders. The public should be able to understand the methods used and how they are implemented and should be able to access the data used to make decisions."

In other words, AMLs are arbitrary and unnecessarily secretive.

Do roundups even work? You don't need a PhD in ecology to see that removing a lot of horses from an area makes it easier for the remaining horses to survive and thrive. The report says roundups are actually compounding, not fixing the problem. They are part of why wild horse and burro populations are flourishing, doubling every four years. (Yet mustang advocates contend that thinning herds will create genetically unhealthy herds. Still others say AMLs aren't low enough and hurt the wildlife populations.)

According to the report, the BLM is spending a lot of money to exacerbate their very mission. What about the cost? Last year, it cost $43 million to keep about fifty thousand horses off the range in short- and long-term holding pens. Less than one in two horses gets adopted. And with slaughter not an option, the U.S. government (or Joe Taxpayer) becomes the biggest horse owner in the world.

The New York Times compared the sprawling stockade numbers to the people population of Cheyenne, Wyoming. That city's annual budget is less than the BLM's budget for dealing with horses and burros. "The continuation of 'business-as-usual' practices will be expensive and unproductive for BLM," the report said.

The report devotes scores of pages to options in fertility control, discussing chemical to surgical options for both stallions and mares. It implores the BLM to address its many challenges, to reduce costs, and improve the welfare of not only the horses and burros but all animals on the range. "Given the nature of the situation, a satisfactory resolution will take time, resources, and dedication to a combination of strategies underpinned by science.

"In the short term, intensive management of free-ranging horses and burros would be expensive, but

256

addressing the problem immediately with a long-term view is probably a more affordable and satisfactory answer than continuing to remove animals to long-term holding facilities. Investing in science-based management approaches would not solve the problem instantly, but it could lead the Wild Horse and Burro Program to a more financially sustainable path that manages healthy horses and burros with greater public confidence."

A Note of Bureau Sympathy

Keep in mind that the BLM must also consider other federal acts pertaining to public lands, including the Federal Land Policy and Management Act, the Wilderness Act, the Clean Water Act, and the Endangered Species Act. A crowded dinner table, indeed, and everyone's hungry and watching the cook. Don't take sides, just use science, they say.

If you're thinking the folks behind this report are just a bunch of wonks from Washington, D. C., think again. The committee includes scientists and veterinarians from Montana, California, Colorado, Utah, Missouri, Nevada, and Washington.

It was, according to chairman and veterinarian Guy Hughes Palmer, an extraordinary effort of collaboration, commitment, and citizen science. He writes,

> "Science alone, even the best science, cannot resolve the divergent viewpoints on how best to manage free-ranging horses and burros on public lands. Evidence-based science can, however, center debate about management options on the basis of confidence in the data, predictable outcomes of specific options, and understanding of both what is known and where uncertainty remains. I am confident that this study

provides a center point and hope that it will serve as a guide for the first step in the journey toward ensuring that genetically viable, physically and behaviorally healthy equid populations can be maintained while preserving a thriving, balanced ecosystem on public lands."

Mustangs – Sidebar

Producer Cindy Meehl will be plenty busy this year as she works with the Unbranded team to develop the documentary film of the three-thousand-mile adventure.

She paused with me to address the complexity of the mustang message. "We're trying to get a real holistic look at the mustang issue, from all sides, not necessarily to point any fingers but just to explain it. Ranchers. BLM. Advocates. Shelters. Holding pens. The whole nine yards. It's a misunderstood issue because you hear sound bites.

"I don't think most people know all the facts about exactly what the process is. So we're trying to do a ton of research and make a really clear picture for the audience without taking sides. I think if there was ever a crisis in the mustang world, it's now. And certainly, it's been brewing for a very long time."

Meehl and a film crew from her Cedar Creek Productions traveled to the National Wild Horse and Burro Advisory Board meeting in Washington, D.C., and interviewed attendees, adding to some four hundred hours of footage.

"I don't know that we see a great answer anywhere but I'm adamant about people not jumping to conclusions based on one news report they heard. It's been misunderstood...I don't want to say 'misrepresented,' but I think it's often not a holistic view," said Meehl.

WANTED, THEN UNWANTED

Mainers think about horse slaughter more than folks from other states. Why? Because they slaughter horses in Canada. The horse slaughter plant in Massueville, Quebec, is a five-hour drive from my former home in Maine.

The other reason Mainers contemplate slaughter is because of our recent tough economic times. It's a poor state made poorer by the Great Recession. When push comes to shove, owners may send their horses into the slaughter stream as an alternative to backyard neglect and starvation.

OK, owners may not knowingly send their horses to slaughter, but don't kid yourself. When a horse is sold or given away, unless it's an extraordinary arrangement, the horse could easily head north.

It's that bad.

From my perspective, it's more productive to discuss the humane treatment of horses, rather than what happens to their bodies after they die. Why? Because many, many more horses are at risk from cruel and neglectful treatment by private owners than as potential slaughter candidates. For every horse sent to slaughter, there are more suffering and waiting to die in pastures.

So how do we improve their situation? Treat the problem at the faucet, not the end of the hose. Restrict breeding and treat horse ownership as a privilege, not a right.

When I lived briefly in Marshfield, Massachusetts, the town's animal control officer was charged with inspecting every horse barn every year. There was no sizeable fee. The town's horse owners were held accountable, just like dog owners. It helped to maintain an equine census, kept a history of all barns, and flagged potential abuse and neglect cases. In the eight years living in that town, there were no cases of cruelty or neglect.

Most horse owners scream and jump up and down when you talk about regulation of ownership and breeding. We'd rather operate with impunity and assume that problems within our horse community will work themselves out on their own. But have you looked around? And have you noticed how little clout we have compared with, say, the state's dog owners? Is it any surprise that advocates for other species scoff at our ways?

If it helped weed out irresponsible breeders and incorrigible owners, I'd welcome oversight. If it could raise funds for education, advocacy, vaccination and gelding clinics, I'm all for it. If we toed the line here as responsible owners, breeders, and neighbors, I doubt we'd have such a massive problem.

Fewer unwanted horses mean fewer heading to slaughter.

Horse Breeding & Slaughter – Sidebar

We watch those horrible news stories about animals being seized from abusive or neglectful owners. We see their thin, dirty bodies and hope that they truly have been saved and will live better lives. But what really happens?

In one specific case, anyway, hats off to the state and the Maine State Society for the Protection of Animals. The Society has saved thousands of lives since it was established in 1872. Just take a walk down the aisles of their Windham barns to see how many presumably wrecked lives have been salvaged.

Brooke is one of them. She came to the MSSPA several years ago after being seized by the state. At the time of the seizure, she was being kept in a stall with three other horses. It was a desperate life.

But at the MSSPA barn, she flourished. Her survivor attitude and zest for life made her an exciting, albeit challenging adoption prospect.

I had the privilege of taking Brooke to a fundraiser for the Maine Equine Welfare Alliance at a Tractor Supply store. She was the MEWA greeter—calm and friendly, accepting all comers, including elderly with walkers, yappy dogs, and excitable toddlers. She handled it all with grace, never pinning her ears back, never acting aggressively, never showing signs of discomfort or anxiety. She stood patiently at the store entrance and took a few breaks to graze on nearby grass.

It was proof positive. Those very horses you might have last seen in a sorry, traumatized state can recover and flourish with love and support.

I'm forever thankful to the MSSPA for saving Brooke and giving her a second chance at a happy, productive life.

POLITICS AND HORSES

Ten years ago, this slow-learner realized something about friendships. And today, I learned all over again.

Back then, I ran several times a week with other stay-at-home moms. Together, we'd run for an hour while a babysitter watched our kids. We'd talk about everything. Run after run, year after year, we'd laugh and share our struggles and successes. It was wonderful camaraderie.

Then one day, during the Clinton impeachment process, we got to talking politics. One friend argued for Clinton. One argued against him. Our pace got faster and faster. The argument became more and more heated. All those years and I'd never realized what deep-seated convictions my girlfriends held—not just about politicians but about the issues behind our political leaders. We headed back to our homes, some of us barely speaking to one another. What an eye-opener!

It happened again. This time, my circle of friends was horsewomen. Now, I'm not politically active by any stretch of the imagination, but I still have my convictions. And when one friend voiced her conviction quite to the contrary, it floored me. How could she think that? What planet is she on? How can we still be friends? I'm sure she wondered the same about me.

But then I thought about the horses. The rants and raves in my head started to subside. Our horses had given us common ground. Who comes first, the husband or the horses? We'd laugh. The horses, of course! We can talk about them for hours without disagreement. We share the same mindset. We like to bond with them. We like to teach them and have them teach us. We like to grow with them. We like to care for them. We're devoted to them.

It was clear from this non-horse exchange that we didn't see eye-to-eye on bigger issues. But if I drop dead tomorrow, I'd want her to be the one caring for my horses. Hands down.

ELEVEN:
Fiction

LILY & JEAN

Jean headed to the barn and whistled. "Lily, let's get out on the trail, huh?"

Lily was the bell mare of the twenty-horse herd at the 3 Bar E. She picked up her head and pricked her ears forward. Jean entered the paddock and moved past a few horses, reached Lily, and paused to stroke her neck.

She was a special horse, born on the same day as Jean's niece, Janey. It was Easter Sunday thirteen years ago. Jean had been there, running from barn to house, fielding calls from the hospital, and helping Lily's mother bring her filly into the world. It'd been one heck of a day for new life.

With Jean's encouragement, Lily had slowly developed into a strong leader. She was a vital member of the ranch staff, keeping track of the herd instinctively and incessantly. She could count her charges faster than any wrangler. She looked after them like a kindergarten teacher looks after her students on a field trip. A never-ending field trip, that is.

Jean brought Lily into the barn, tossed the lead line over a half-wall, and grabbed a brush and a hoof pick. Lily shuffled her angle to look out at the herd. When Jean picked up one of her front hooves, Lily touched the woman's lower back with her muzzle.

"Yup," answered Jean. "We're heading out. Just you and me."

Jean filled two Nalgene bottles with water from the tack room sink and tossed them into the worn saddlebags.

They moved out of the barn and away from the paddock. Lily whinnied. Several horses turned their heads and answered, then bowed their heads to continue grazing. Lily whinnied again and pranced nervously, not used to leaving alone. Jean tightened the girth and mounted. It felt good, Jean thought, even if she was getting old and perpetually sore. Her tanned, rough, and wrinkled hands stroked Lily's neck.

Most days, the two were consumed with ranch duties: moving cattle, checking fences. Only occasionally did Jean have the time and energy for a pleasure ride. And when it happened, it was always a welcome respite, a getaway, a reminder of how good they had it.

She checked her saddle. She carried rain gear, bear spray, and a folding eight-inch knife with a serrated blade. She often used the knife for impromptu trailblazing. But the rain gear and bear spray? Never used them. Oh, once she accidentally set off the bear spray. Most unpleasant. Bear spray, sold in a slender, 10-inch aerosol can, is a jumbo unit of Mace.

Last summer, she released the spray trigger while helping a ranch guest with his saddle. It got her right between the eyes. Instant pain and blindness! She spent the next hour in the bathroom, flushing her eyes with warm water over and over and over and over until the pain subsided and sight returned. At least she knew it worked.

With a gentle nudge, Jean turned her horse and headed toward the old logging road leading into Towas National Forest. Lily looked back and stepped sideways.

"Stop it, girl," Jean answered with a squeeze of her thighs. "We'll be back in no time."

With her legs, her hands, and her voice, Jean won the argument and the two moved smoothly away from the ranch. They both looked through the forest, where the light filtered down through large evergreens and bounced off exposed rocks. Squirrels flitted out of sight. Woodpeckers flew casually from dead tree to dead tree. It was cooler and quieter, and the light was softer in the woods.

Jean maintained a steady dialogue with Lily. It was a strategy she'd used since she was a girl to calm and distract her horse. Heck, it'd been a way to calm and distract herself in those days when she had less faith in her abilities.

But then something interrupted the conversation. Or, rather, it was the lack of something that interrupted the conversation. All of a sudden, things were still. The birds stopped chattering. The quiet gave Jean and Lily pause. Jean leaned back slightly and pulled up her horse to a halt.

They looked around the woods and then peered into the shadows of the forest. They listened. The tops of the trees rustled, but there was little else. Not even the squirrels chittered.

Then, a hundred feet ahead, there was a rush of brown from behind a downed tree. Then a cat yowled and Jean saw a flash of a mountain lion. Two big masses—one tan and one nearly black rushed off at opposite angles.

Lily coiled underneath her, obedient but urgent in her desire to flee. She listened to Jean who was silently telling her to stay put. She and Lily (an agitated Lily who pranced slightly in her place) watched the big animals sprint through the trees. They bobbed and angled like combat soldiers dodging bullets. "All right, girl," said Jean in as soothing a voice as she could manage. "They're gone. For now, anyway."

She wondered what the predators had been doing right before she and her horse spooked them. Jean asked Lily to move off the trail toward the spot where she had first seen the cat and bear. They walked through underbrush and over a few downed trees. Ten yards ahead, she spotted a freshly-killed deer. She dismounted and got a better look. It was a big buck, a nine-pointer weighing over two hundred pounds, she guessed. She couldn't tell from the wounds which animal had killed it. She was no game warden and, to be honest, she didn't quite have the stomach for it this day.

It took a few seconds to figure out what had just whizzed before their eyes. But here's what happened, Jean theorized: the bear had likely killed it. Then a mountain lion had come across the bear and his prize and was attempting to fight for a piece of it when Jean and Lily showed up. It could have been the other way around, with the bear smelling out the cat's prize; Jean wasn't sure.

She was sure that if they had been hungrier, more desperate, or just plain meaner, the predators might have stayed to defend and claim the carcass. But, this time anyway, neither did.

They got back on the trail. Lily automatically started back toward the ranch to return to her herd. "Oh, honey," said Jean, smiling. "Just because we started off rough, doesn't mean we're throwing in the towel."

Convincing her horse, of course, meant convincing herself even as her hands involuntarily shook and she stomached a wave of nausea. It was the backside of an adrenalin rush, and she wondered if Lily might be feeling the same sensation.

Jean's mother, long dead, appeared in her mind. A wide-brimmed straw hat covered her eyes. Her pants, loose and worn, were cinched up with thick black belt. The big, turquoise-embellished, silver buckle shone in the dusty light of Jean's recollection. Her mother was casually running her fingers through the scruffy mane of their old pony, Caesar. She placed her other hand gently on Jean's shoulder.

"Horses will feed off you and you will feed off your horses," she heard her mother's words from decades ago. "Think of yourselves as plugged into one another—not like a truck and trailer. More like Siamese twins. You don't haul this pony out for a ride, Jean. You agree to it. You're the leader, but you move as a pair."

What was true then is true now.

Jean and Lily moved on, as partners. She took a full breath and blew it out slowly. She sat more deeply in her seat and stroked Lily's neck. "I'm your lightning rod and you're mine, aren't you?" Jean said.

Lily dropped her head. The loose reins swung gently from side to side. They followed an old logging path through a meadow full of high grass and wildflowers. The meadow was the size of a football field. They reached the end, where pine trees marked the beginning of a pleasant climb.

Her mother came back into view. This time, the belt was off and the big buckle was being swung across Jean's butt. She was a stubborn, strong-willed, ignorant eight year old, and she'd been arguing with her pony. Caesar was tolerating her tantrum, standing obediently as Jean smacked him with the reins and yelled at him for stepping on her new cowboy boots.

Her mother had watched the spectacle from the big bay window of the kitchen and marched across the ranch driveway, whipping her belt through pant loops as she advanced. "Caesar is getting beat for no good reason," she told Jean in a low and steady voice that belied her swift actions. "You are getting beat for mistreating him." The punishment was swift and shocking. After three whacks, her mother released, looked her in the eye, and asked, "Do you understand?"

Jean nodded yes, fighting back tears. Her mother let go of Jean's arm and walked back into the house.

Lily lifted her head and perked her ears at two squirrels chasing each other through the deadfall. Jean stroked her mare's neck again and refocused on the path ahead. They zigzagged up hairpin turns and climbed a ridge. They loped through Clark's Meadow (so named by the locals because the Lewis & Clark National Historic Trail passed through it) and after twenty minutes entered thicker woods.

Both of their bodies started to relax. Lily lowered her head and maintained her powerful walk without any coaxing. Now and again, Jean observed, Lily paused to pick up a distinct smell. They walked on through the tightening trail up the mountainside. Lily picked her head up and stopped short.

"I didn't ask you to stop," said Jean. She looked around and urged Lily with her legs. Lily didn't budge. Jean followed her line of sight and then saw what Lily had seen ten seconds ago and undoubtedly smelled a half-mile back.

It was a grizzly cub, foraging on huckleberries not one hundred yards to their right. This winter's baby, no doubt. Darn cute. The fuzzy brown ball moved clumsily through the thick bushes, consumed with its consumption.

Jean's immediate thought was: "Where's Mom?"

Lily shifted and snapped a branch underfoot. The cub lifted its head, spotted the pair, and gave a little moan, calling his mother.

She shortened her reins, tried to sit deep in the saddle and sink her heels, silently telling Lily to freeze but be ready.

Jean looked uphill. Then she heard Mama Bear, grunting and moving through the underbrush toward her cub from two hundred yards away. Had she seen us yet? Maybe not, but I bet she smells us, thought Jean.

She reached for the bear spray, tied to the saddle with leather straps just in front of her thigh. Lily shifted.

"Stand, girl."

They saw bears often but mostly smaller black bears, mostly from a distance. They'd never, in their ten years riding together, had such a close encounter, and they had never been so miserably sandwiched between a grizzly mother and her cub.

Jean struggled with the leather tie. She'd cinched the can there in April and hadn't messed with it since then. The knot was rigid and encrusted with dirt. Lily pranced in place.

Was it like writing a check while driving? Like tying a kicking toddler's shoe? No, it was like doing both at the same time with a gun to your head, she thought. She cursed her thick fingers and cursed the tough leather straps.

"Jesus, Lily. Stand," Jean whispered forcefully.

The bear mother saw them now. She jogged toward them, building speed. Jean freed the knot at last. The can nearly slipped to the ground as she grabbed it. She fumbled to remove the safety tab. In those few seconds, the mother had closed to within seventy feet.

"Okay, Lily, not quite a bear sandwich. Mom at ten o'clock. Baby at three o'clock. That makes our escape route behind us." Jean spoke in a staccato voice as if rattling off the morning orders to her ranch hands. The delivery made it clear what needed to be done.

The bears advanced. Jean considered the Mace. This was the thing with bear spray: it sprayed only thirty feet or so. So if a bear was threatening you, it REALLY needed to threaten you. Bad-breath-range, friends had joked.

Jean quickly scanned behind them. It was typical forest floor, full of thickets, downed trees, saplings fighting with established trees for space. Two hundred yards on, the trail worked its way downhill.

She weighed the odds. Stand or flee? Given the forest growth, Mama Bear could easily out-sprint Lily. But did they really want to stand their ground?

Jean signaled Lily and the mare instantly pivoted on her haunches and trotted powerfully through the thick underbrush.

She moved assertively and authoritatively, despite stumbling and tripping over deadfall. Jean counted on Lily to navigate unassisted toward the trail, so she could turn around in the saddle and focus on the mother bear. Thick branches struck Jean in the upper body and head. One knocked off her hat, a decade-old rustler's brim she cherished. It bounced off Lily's hind quarters and dropped onto the top of a shoulder-high evergreen, giving the sapling the look of a lonely wrangler in the middle of nowhere. The mother bear paused for a half-second to inspect it and then continued her pursuit.

Jean glanced forward. In another fifty yards, they'd be on the path. Mother Bear picked up her pace, moving easily through the brush that was so treacherous for Jean and Lily. Shit, thought Jean, maybe there's something to that stand-and-fight philosophy. The bears seemed to enjoy the pursuit, and they were closing the gap.

Jean held the bear spray over Lily's rump and depressed the tab, hoping the bears might run into its mist and be deterred. At last, they reached the path. Jean moved her reins up Lily's neck and adjusted her seat. The mare surged underneath her.

Galloping in an arena can be fun. The footing is sound. You can open up your horse and run for all it's worth. No obstacles except the predictable ones, like barrels. But this galloping was fleeing, and there wasn't anything fun, pretty or predictable about it. Lily wanted to go. Jean wanted to stay in the saddle. The horse tripped on roots and skittered over rocks. A few times, Jean lost her balance and lurched forward, catching the saddle's horn under her ribs. It smarted.

In less than a minute, Jean could see that the bears couldn't be bothered with continuing. (Not that the Mace mist had deterred them.) They had chugged to a stop and watched horse and rider from the path's edge.

Jean and Lily ran on. They reached Clark's Meadow and opened up to a full gallop with no roots, branches or boulders to impede them. As they approached the woods again, Jean struggled to bring Lily back to a trot. She pulled her up and moved her around to face the meadow.

"You're alright, Lily. You're alright." Jean laughed when she realized she was still clutching the bear spray. She reset the safety and tied it back to the saddle as Lily bobbed her head, not content to stand.

They walked the last few miles and paused at a stream for Lily to drink. Jean drank from her Nalgene bottle. How did they get so thirsty? She stroked her mare's sweaty neck and resumed their conversation. Both glanced frequently back up the logging road.

"You know we're going to have to get back there to get that hat of mine, don't you? It is my favorite…Relax, girl…We done good today."

BUTTON

This story was originally submitted to the National Public Radio contest, Three Minute Fiction. *The contest rules stipulated that writers use the words **plant**, **trick**, **fly**, and **button** and that the piece be no more than 600 hundred words.*

"Button," said the old man, "as in cute as a button." He twirled a toothpick between his lips and kicked at a weed in his dirt driveway. The visitor admired the pony as she moved lightly around the paddock.

Button seemed to match the feed store ad, all right:

RETIRED CIRCUS PONY READY FOR A NEW LIFE

GREY IN COLOR BUT NOT IN SPIRIT

FREE TO A GOOD HOME

"I'm not looking for anything fancy, just someone to have fun with," the visitor shared.

"Oh, I expect she'll be perfect for you," said the man, who had his back turned as he had grabbed a halter and headed toward the pony.

They discussed Button's care and feed. Already smitten, the visitor listened to the man's instructions as she stroked the pony's mane and neck. "She's an easy keeper," he said. He looked at the pony with a smile. Did they just exchange glances? Button swished her tail.

"Just give her a handful of grain in the morning and the same at night. Oh, and she's not too keen on bugs. You'd best have some of this." He handed the visitor a half-used container of fly spray. "Go ahead. Sure, I won't be needing it."

The man helped load the pony into the shiny horse trailer and shook hands earnestly with Button's new owner.

At the woman's request, he even took pictures with her little digital camera: the woman, with a big smile, her eyes fixed on her new charge. The pony, poking her head out of the trailer's little window. The woman offered her a handful of grass. Button chewed it and licked her lips. He snapped the picture.

The image showed Button sticking out her tongue. "Hold on." The man smirked. "That one won't do. We'll take another."

The next day came and it was time for their first ride. The attentive rider brushed Button's dappled coat and lovingly combed her mane and tail. She fitted the saddle and tightened the girth. She slipped on the bridle, adjusted and readjusted the leather straps.

Button stood serenely as the woman mounted up. The rider rode cautiously at first, like a newly-licensed driver with a new car, making sure everything was in good working order, making sure they had a good understanding between them.

They moved through the woods as the birds chirped and flitted from tree to tree. Button was lively but obedient. "What a lucky find!" exclaimed the woman. From the woods to the clearing, the pair crossed the countryside. The rider relaxed, let slack the reins, and daydreamed of the summer ahead, of blissful, harmonious rides. Maybe they could ride clear to the shore and go swimming together!

The pony felt the ease of her rider's legs across her back. She noticed the rider's slow breathing and loose hands. All of a sudden, the pony flicked her tail and kicked out at a passing plant. Like all the other plants along this stretch, it was ripe with bugs and insects. The bugs rose in protest. The pony jumped sideways. The rider plopped to the ground. 'Trick,' thought the pony as she licked her lips and snatched a mouthful of grass. 'As in trick pony.'

THE LONG HAUL BACK

With a clean rag, Oscar ran his hand across the fine lettering, ERIE FEELING. He'd painted the name in elegant, gold script across the stern of his small barge. It was a nod to the old canal near his childhood home. Like any decent boat name, it had a double entendre.

Oscar looked over the barge and smiled broadly. His pride—the thing born of years of hard, impassioned craftsmanship—now started to bubble up from his toes. He was beaming. Inside, he was bursting. His heart beat at twice its normal rate. He had to remember to breathe.

Upon retirement five years ago, he said goodbye to Pennsylvania and a successful corporate career. He and his wife, Lou, were fulfilling a dream of ex-patriot living in France. He had traded white collar for white wine and loved it.

Oscar was ready to go. All the bits of his final checklist had been ticked off.

"Looks great, honey," said his wife, Lou. "She's gorgeous. The carvings and trim work, especially."

He readied the donkeys' stalls with hay and water, then loaded the donkeys. If he was going to do it, Oscar planned several years ago, he was going to do it right. No motors to push them back up river. Their diminutive donkeys, Napo and Leon, would do the job.

He finished loading up for the maiden voyage. Lou embellished his supplies with extra wine and fruit, carrots for the donkeys, treats for the dog.

Oscar nervously directed his crew. "*Allons-y!*"

At Oscar's signal, their friend and neighbor, Raoul, untied the bowline, and then the stern line, tossing the thick hemp cords aboard. The two men waved zealous goodbyes, a bit overzealous perhaps as they were still close enough to reach across the water and shake hands.

"*Au revoir, mes amis!*" said Raoul.

They were off. Lou even took off her neckerchief, laughed, and waved it dramatically. Yank, the dog, barked exuberantly and wagged his tail, thumping it against one of the portholes.

Oscar breathed. And then, as if for the first time, he saw the bridge. It hung over the river, just around the big bend, half a mile downstream from their home. Lou and Oscar had admired it during countless walks. Built five hundred years ago, Raoul had told them, with mammoth boulders carved perfectly to shape. Its graceful, arcing curve made the river that much more beautiful, they had agreed. It was a treasure to behold.

But in an arrogant, ignorant instant, Oscar hated it. "Lou! Lou!" he screamed. "The bridge! *Le pont! Le sacre pont!* That blessed bridge!"

Lou didn't need to see it to know. Instinctively, she moved back to the stern, closer to Oscar.

"The cabin," he said, in between moans and whimpers. "I don't think the cabin will go under it."

He calculated furiously. They traveled the speed of the river. In this region, that meant at a brisk walking pace. Given the distance, they had five minutes, maybe six, to avoid disaster or worse: utter, sincere, and stereotypical American buffoonery. He could hear the locals cackling already.

"OK, here's what we're going to do," Oscar meted out his frantic plan. "Help me with Napo and Leon."

Oscar moved toward their stalls, grabbed their harnesses and lines, tacked them up hastily, and moved them onto the deck. They were the size of Shetland ponies, but Oscar, in his adrenalized state, lifted them up and into the water, tossing them like wriggling oil drums into the river.

He stripped off his boots, Cleveland Indians cap, and denim shirt, and dove in after them, gripping their harness lines. For an instant, the bewildered animals thrashed back toward the barge. But when Oscar joined them and started swimming to shore, they turned and headed with him.

Oscar reached the river's edge and bounded onto the old dirt path running alongside the river, gently cajoling the soaking donkeys by the reins and pleading with them to trot. Napo and Leon obliged. In another minute, he had secured their lines and waited until the ERIE FEELING drew them taut. Lou watched and manned the lines on board, glancing ahead and then back to her sopping, pathetic, frenetic husband.

"OK, Oscar, ask them to move out," Lou yelled.

"*Allons-y!*" he called. (Purchased from Raoul's cousin, they understood only French commands.) Napo and Leon strained against the lines. Oscar pulled, too. Together, they stepped. Backward.

"*Allons-y! Allons-y!*" Oscar grabbed the lines between the donkeys and the barge and attempted to lighten their load. Still, the threesome shuffled actively backward.

Closer and closer, they inched toward the bridge. It seemed to grow in size as they approached—bigger in every way but height. By now, one hundred feet away, Oscar could see that the cabin would indeed be too high. By six inches perhaps. Six inches of finely sanded, detailed, oiled, and caressed mahogany. Might as well as have been six feet.

The ERIE FEELING flowed gracefully, defiantly, majestically toward her doom.

On shore, the three creatures strained against the ropes. The ropes strained. On board, Lou cheered them on frantically. Yank yipped incessantly. Alerted by the commotion, Raoul raced through his field and joined Oscar on the dirt path. Together they pulled and shouted and pulled some more.

The ERIE FEELING continued her proud pace. The slow, cacophonous, reverse parade approached within feet of the bridge. From her station in the stern, Lou could see the hewn stone from a new perspective. It was indeed terribly beautiful.

And then, the ERIE FEELING, the river, and all the involved beings reached a brief détente. The current seemed to ease.

The donkeys and men redoubled their efforts. The barge stopped and then ever-so-slightly reversed course. "*Oui! Oui! Allons-y, mes amis!*" cried Raoul to the donkeys.

Oscar didn't dare looked downriver and instead dug his chin into his sweaty chest, grunted loudly, and soldiered forward several shuffling steps.

"You're doing it, guys!" cried Lou. "She's coming back!"

Their few minutes of glorious downriver travel replayed now as forty minutes of agonizing retreat. Oscar plodded step by step with his tiring donkeys, imploring them to make the final stretch.

When they reached the dock, Raoul wrapped the lines around the cinches and doubled the knots, just to be sure. Lou and Yank disembarked. The three of them collapsed in the folding chairs. Oscar shook his head, wiped sweat off his brow, and replaced his cap. "Home again the same day, Lou," panted Oscar. "If you can't cry, then laugh. We didn't lose her, did we?"

He laughed. It was hearty and rich with relief. Lou and Raoul looked over to the man to be sure he meant it. They smiled and laughed and cheered too. It was a victory cheer. Of sorts.

CITATIONS AND REFERENCES
(in order)

Beston, Henry. *The Outermost Horse*. Henry Holt and Company, LLC. New York, 1949. Print

Corson, Trevor. The Secret Life of Lobsters. Harper Perennial, New York. 2005. Print.

Julie Goodnight, Q & A on crossties:
http://juliegoodnight.com/questionsNew.php?id=131

Dr. Sue McDonnell, Q & A on bolting:
http://www.thehorse.com/articles/32026/rehabbing-the-bolter?utm_source=Newsletter&utm_medium=welfare-industry&utm_campaign=07-04-2013

Peter Gould, Breaking Bad interview:
http://www.npr.org/2013/10/03/228813142/breaking-bad-writers-this-is-it-theres-no-more

Palmer, Brian, "How Dangerous is Asthma?" Slate Magazine.
http://www.slate.com/articles/news_and_politics/explainer/2012/02/anthony_shadid_s_death_how_dangerous_is_asthma_.html

Namanny, David, "A Safe Return to Osage: Four local soldiers welcomed home" Mitchell County Press News.
http://globegazette.com/mcpress/news/local/a-safe-return-to-osage-four-local-soldiers-welcomed-home/article_9721t62b-41e2-5c75-8d91-9ce92c083c85.html

Lauren Fraser's piece on a field crisis appears courtesy of Lauren Fraser. http://goodhorsemanship.ca/

More information on Evidence-Based Horsemanship can be found at http://www.evidence-basedhorsemanship.com/

More information in the International Society of Equitation Science can be found at http://www.equitationscience.com/
Black, Martin. "Thoughts on catching a horse" Eclectic Horseman Magazine, edition 65, May/June 2012.

Grandin, Temple; Catherine Johnson. *Animals in Translation*, Scribner, New York. 2005. Paperback.

Los Angeles Times editorial, "End the Killer Whale Circus" http://www.latimes.com/news/opinion/editorials/la-ed-killer-whale-20130801,0,6263962.story#axzz2tzvyayBC

Frans de Waal, "Brains of the Animal Kingdom" Wall Street Journal, March 22, 2013. http://online.wsj.com/news/articles/SB10001424127887323869604578370574285382756?mg=reno64-wsj&url=http%3A%2F%2Fonline.wsj.com%2Farticle%2FSB100014241278873238696045783 70574285382756.html

Budiansky, Stephen, *The Nature of Horses: Their Evolution, Intelligence, and Behaviour.* 1998. Orion Publishing Group, Ltd. London. Print.
Alexsandrova, Natalija, "Thermoregulation of horses in a cold time of year" http://www.academialiberti.de/en/articles/read/22/Thermoregulation-in-horses-in-a-cold-time-of-year/

Whip Use study, 9th International Society of Equitation Science Proceedings, p. 54. http://www.equitationscience.com/documents/Conferences/2013/9th_IS ES_Proceedings.pdf

Barrel Racing Study, Karen Waite et al. Michigan State University.
http://besthorsepractices.com/details-of-barrel-racing-study/

Voice Study, Nottingham Trent University, 8th International Society of
Equitation Science Proceedings,
http://www.equitationscience.com/documents/Conferences/ISESConfere
nceProceedings2012.pdf

Dr. David W. Ramey, What's in Your Supplement,
http://www.doctorramey.com/whats-in-your-supplement/

The National Academies Press: Using Science to Improve the Wild Horse
and Burro Program. The Way Forward. June, 2013.
http://www.nap.edu/catalog.php?record_id=13511

ACKNOWLEDGMENTS

I thank Emily Kitching, president of Eclectic Horseman,
for generously writing the foreword.

For the cover and author photographs as well as some additional
chapter images, I thank Shepherd Waldenberger. Thanks go to Sally
Butcher, Agnes Moyon, and Steve Peters for additional photos. For
content contributions, I thank Bobby Fantarella, Lauren Fraser, Joel
Nelson, and Sam Butcher.

For manuscript help, I thank Cindy Meehl of Cedar Creek
Productions, Meris Bickford of the Maine State Society for the
Protection of Animals, and especially Gary Lawless, poet and owner
of Gulf of Maine books.

Thanks to Susan Giffin for her kind, patient, and accurate editing.

I'm indebted to my friends, family, and especially the readers of
NickerNews and *BestHorsePractices* for their excellent enthusiasm and
constructive criticism over the years. Thanks, too, to the countless
interviewees – horse folks, vets, researchers, and others who allowed
me to query them in the pursuit of knowledge and opinion.

And warm thanks to Steve Peters for his steadfast support and
encouragement throughout all stages of this book's development.

CPSIA information can be obtained at www.ICGtesting.com
Printed in the USA
BVOW01s1302110414

350178BV00002B/2/P

9 781600 479540